Key to Success

in Context

Level 3

A Curriculum for

- Summer School
- After School
- Exploration Programs

HOLT, RINEHART AND WINSTON

Mathematics in Context is a comprehensive curriculum for the middle grades.
It was developed in 1991 through 1997 in collaboration with the Wisconsin Center
for Education Research, School of Education, University of Wisconsin-Madison and
the Freudenthal Institute at the University of Utrecht, The Netherlands, with the
support of the National Science Foundation Grant No. 9054928.

The revision of the curriculum was carried out in 2003 through 2005, with the
support of the National Science Foundation Grant No. ESI 0137414.

National Science Foundation

Opinions expressed are those of the authors
and not necessarily those of the Foundation.

ISBN 0-03-073092-9

3 4 5 6   073   09 08 07

The *Mathematics in Context* Development Team

Development 1991–1997

The initial versions of the lessons in this material were developed by members of the following staffs.

Wisconsin Center for Education

Research Staff

Thomas A. Romberg
Director

Joan Daniels Pedro
Assistant to the Director

Gail Burrill
Coordinator

Margaret R. Meyer
Coordinator

Project Staff

Jonathan Brendefur
Laura Brinker
James Browne
Jack Burrill
Rose Byrd
Peter Christiansen
Barbara Clarke
Doug Clarke
Beth R. Cole
Fae Dremock
Mary Ann Fix

Sherian Foster
James A, Middleton
Jasmina Milinkovic
Margaret A. Pligge
Mary C. Shafer
Julia A. Shew
Aaron N. Simon
Marvin Smith
Stephanie Z. Smith
Mary S. Spence

Freudenthal Institute Staff

Jan de Lange
Director

Els Feijs
Coordinator

Martin van Reeuwijk
Coordinator

Mieke Abels
Nina Boswinkel
Frans van Galen
Koeno Gravemeijer
Marja van den
  Heuvel-Panhuizen
Jan Auke de Jong
Vincent Jonker
Ronald Keijzer
Martin Kindt

Jansie Niehaus
Nanda Querelle
Anton Roodhardt
Leen Streefland
Adri Treffers
Monica Wijers
Astrid de Wild

Revision 2003–2006

The revised versions of the lessons in this material were developed by members of the following staffs.

Wisconsin Center for Education

Research Staff

Thomas A. Romberg
Director

David C. Webb
Coordinator

Gail Burrill
Editorial Coordinator

Margaret A. Pligge
Editorial Coordinator

Freudenthal Institute Staff

Jan de Lange
Director

Truus Dekker
Coordinator

Mieke Abels
Content Coordinator

Monica Wijers
Content Coordinator

Project Staff

Sarah Ailts
Beth R. Cole
Erin Hazlett
Teri Hedges
Karen Hoiberg
Carrie Johnson
Jean Krusi
Elaine McGrath

Margaret R. Meyer
Anne Park
Bryna Rappaport
Kathleen A. Steele
Ana C. Stephens
Candace Ulmer
Jill Vettrus

Arthur Bakker
Peter Boon
Els Feijs
Dédé de Haan
Martin Kindt

Nathalie Kuijpers
Huub Nilwik
Sonia Palha
Nanda Querelle
Martin van Reeuwijk

◆ Contents

Dear Student,

Welcome to *Mathematics in Context Key to Success!*

MiC Key to Success encourages you to think about mathematics in new and different ways. You will notice that the math problems are presented in a realistic context. Your teacher will introduce the context and encourage you to develop your own informal strategies to solve the problems. You may find clues for math tools you might use, or you may find hints in the pictures or wording of the problems, but you will not find one specific way to solve the problem.

As you progress through each lesson's activities, you will begin to understand how this method of learning mathematics will help you develop reasoning and problem-solving skills that you can use next year in math class and in other ways as well.

Most of the problems can be solved and explained in more than one way. You will have opportunities to use manipulatives in math lab-type activities; calculators may be used to help you solve many of the problems. To give you more opportunities to explain your thinking and understand other students' strategies, you will be asked to share your ideas and to listen as other students share their solutions. The goal of this sharing is to decide whether some strategies work better than other strategies to solve particular problems.

You are going to learn about many different mathematical topics while using this program. We hope you find this program to be challenging, exciting, and most of all, fun! The goal is that you learn to make sense of mathematics and have great success!

Sincerely,

The Mathematics in Context Development Team

Key to Success

BRITANNICA
Mathematics
in
Context

Level 3

Lesson
One
Activities

Base Ten

Hieroglyphics

Step back in time to a world without computers, calculators, and television; to Egypt around 3000 B.C.

At this time, Horus was the best stone carver of his village.

He carved little pictures called hieroglyphs to record information.

Here is his latest work. The hieroglyphs on the stone represent the number 1,333,331.

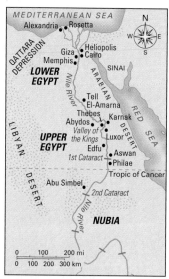

This hieroglyph is an astonished man. Perhaps he is astonished

because he represents a very large number.

1. What number does the astonished man represent?

Here is the number 3,544 written in hieroglyphics.

2. How would Horus write your age? And 1,234?

Today, we use the Arabic system and the **numerals** 0, 1, 2, 3, 4, 5, 6, 7, 8, and 9 to represent any number.

3. Complete the table on **Student Activity Sheet 1** to compare the Egyptian hieroglyphs with the Arabic numerals we use today.

Egyptian Hieroglyph	Egyptian Description	Arabic Numeral	English Word
|	vertical stroke	1	one
∩	a heel bone		
ℰ	a coil or rope		
𐦲	lotus flower		
𐦡	pointing finger		
𓆐	tadpole		
𓁨	an astonished man		

4. What number is represented in this drawing?

5. How would Horus write 420? And 402?

6. How many Egyptian hieroglyphs do you need to draw the number 999?

The Egyptian number system was not well suited for decimal or fraction notation. The decimal notation we use today was developed almost 4,000 years later. A Dutch mathematician, Simon Stevin, invented the decimal point.

7. a. Explain the value of each **digit** in the number 12.574.

    b. Write $7 \times 100 + 6 \times 1 + 4 \times \frac{1}{10} + 5 \times \frac{1}{1000}$ as a single number.

If you multiply a decimal number by 10, the value of each digit is multiplied by 10.

Consider the product of 57.38 × 10.

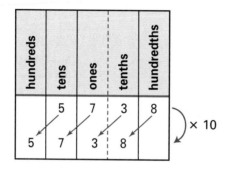

$57.38 \times 10 = 573.8$

$$57.38 = 5 \times \mathbf{10} \ + 7 \times \mathbf{1} \ + 3 \times \frac{\mathbf{1}}{\mathbf{10}} + 8 \times \frac{\mathbf{1}}{\mathbf{100}}$$

$$573.8 \ = 5 \times \mathbf{100} + 7 \times \mathbf{10} + 3 \times \mathbf{1} \ + 8 \times \frac{\mathbf{1}}{\mathbf{10}}$$

$\Big) \times 10$

8. Calculate each product without using a calculator.

    a. 4.8 × 10

    b. 4.8 × 10 × 10

    c. 6.37 × 10 × 10

    d. 9.8 × 10 × 10 × 10

    e. 1.25 × 1,000

    f. 0.57892 × 1,000

Large Numbers

Numerals	Words
1	one
10	ten
100	one hundred
1,000	one thousand
10,000	ten thousand
100,000	one hundred thousand
1,000,000	one million
10,000,000	ten million
100,000,000	one hundred million
1,000,000,000	one billion
10,000,000,000	ten billion
100,000,000,000	one hundred billion
1,000,000,000,000	one trillion

In 2004, the population of the United States was about 292 million, and the world population was about 6 billion.

9. Write these populations using only numerals.

Notice that commas separate each group of three digits. This makes the numbers easy to read. You read the number 2,638,577 as "two million, six hundred thirty-eight thousand, five hundred seventy-seven."

10. How do you read 4,370,000? And 1,500,000,000?

There are different ways to read and write large numbers. For example, you can read 3,200,000 as: "three million, two hundred thousand" or simply as "3.2 million."

11. Write at least two different ways you can read each number.

    a. 6,500,000

    b. 500 million

    c. 1.2 thousand

    d. 750,000

12. Find each product and write your answers using only words.

    a. One million times ten

    b. One hundred times one hundred

    c. One thousand times one thousand

13. **a.** How many thousands are in one million?

    b. How many thousands are in one billion?

    c. How many millions are in one billion?

    d. Use numbers such as 10, 100, 1,000, and so on, to write five different multiplication problems for which the answer is 1,000,000.

14. Suppose you counted from one to one million and every count would last one second. How long would this take?

Exponential Notation

To save time writing zeroes and counting zeroes, scientists invented a special notation, called **exponential notation.**

The number 1,000 written in exponential notation is 10^3 (read as "ten raised to the third **power**" or "ten to the third").

$$1,000 = 10^3 \text{ because } 1,000 = 10 \times 10 \times 10$$

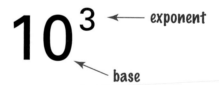

In 10^3, the 10 is the **base**, and the 3 is the **exponent**.

15. Write each number in exponential notation.

    a. 100   **b.** 1,000,000,000   **c.** 10,000,000,000

16. Write each number in numerals and words.

    a. 10^4 **b.** 10^1 **c.** 10^6

Egyptian Hieroglyph	Egyptian Description	Arabic Numeral	English Word
|	vertical stroke	1	One
∩	a heel bone		
ℓ	a coil or rope		
(lotus flower symbol)	lotus flower		
(pointing finger symbol)	pointing finger		
(tadpole/bird symbol)	tadpole		
(astonished man symbol)	an astonished man		

Words	Numeral
Words	**Numeral**
One Thousand	1,000
One Million	1,000,000
One Billion	1,000,000,000
One Trillion	1,000,000,000,000

1. Write the following numbers as a numeral using digits.

    a. thirteen million _____

    b. 2 billion _____

    c. one and a half million _____

    d. 1.4 million _____

    e. 2.3 billion _____

2. And now the other way around, write each number in words.

    a. 7,000,000 _____

    b. 9,000,000,000 _____

    c. 15,000,000 _____

    d. 1,500,000 _____

    e. 5,000,000,000 _____

    f. 500,000 _____

3. Make up a similar writing exercise. Exchange with a classmate and do each other's problems.

On the Number Line

Here are some population data.

1. Next to each label, write the population as numeral using digits.

Australia
19.9 million

Spain
40.3 million

United States
293.0 million

Canada
32.5 million

Cyprus
$\frac{1}{4}$ million

Mexico
105.9 million

World
6.5 billion

120,000,000
115,000,000
110,000,000
105,000,000
100,000,000
95,000,000
90,000,000
85,000,000
80,000,000
75,000,000
70,000,000
65,000,000
60,000,000
55,000,000
50,000,000
45,000,000
40,000,000
35,000,000
30,000,000
25,000,000
20,000,000
15,000,000
10,000,000
5,000,000
0

Source: http://www.census.gov

2. Connect each label to the correct place on the number line. For two labels, this will not be possible; the number line is not long enough.

3. On top of this page, paste a blank sheet of paper. Then extend the number line so that you can connect the label of the United States.

4. Look now at the label of the WORLD. How many extra sheets of paper do you need to connect this label? Explain your answer.

Key to Success

BRITANNICA
Mathematics
in
Context

Level 3

Lesson Two Activities

Prime Numbers

Upside-Down Trees

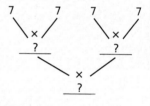

As I was going to St. Ives,
I met a man with seven wives.
Every wife had seven sacks,
Every sack had seven cats,
Every cat had seven kits.
Kits, cats, sacks, and wives,
How many were going to St. Ives?

1. Use an **arithmetic tree** to calculate 2 × 5 × 7 × 7.

Here are two different arithmetic trees to calculate 5 × 5 × 2 × 6 × 3.

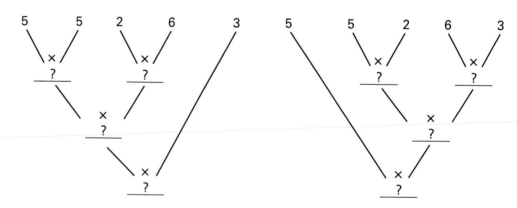

2. a. Will they both give the same result? Why or why not?

   b. Which arithmetic tree would you prefer to use? Why?

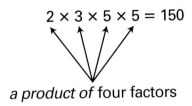

$2 \times 3 \times 5 \times 5 = 150$

a product of four factors

You can write 150 as a product of two factors.

$$150 = 3 \times 50$$

Both numbers, 3 and 50, are factors of 150.

3. a. Explain why 10 is a factor of 150.

   b. What is a factor? Use your own words to describe "factor."

An upside-down arithmetic tree can help you to write a number as a **product of factors**.

4. a. What information does the upside-down arithmetic tree give you?

   b. Use the "end numbers" (the numbers at the end of the tree) to write 24 as a product of factors.

These special arithmetic trees are called **factor trees**. In these factor trees, you will only see multiplication signs. Here is the beginning of a factor tree for the number 1,560.

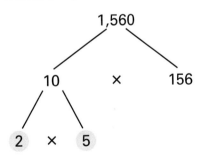

5. a. Copy and complete the factor tree for the number 1,560. Take the branches out as far as possible.

   b. How will you know when you are completely finished with the tree?

   c. Use the end numbers to write 1,560 as a product of factors.

   d. Would you use the number 1 as an end number? Why or why not?

Primes

The end numbers of all factor trees are **prime numbers**. Prime numbers have exactly two factors, the number one and the number itself.

Numbers that are not prime numbers are called **composite numbers**. The number 1 is neither a prime number, nor a composite number.

The ancient Greeks used prime numbers. Eratosthenes discovered a method to extract all of the prime numbers from 1 to 100. Beginning with a list of 100 numbers, he sifted out the prime numbers by crossing off multiples of numbers.

The **multiples** of 2 are 2, 4, 6, 8, 10, and so on.

6. **a.** What is the next multiple of 2?

    b. List the first five multiples of 3.

    c. Are there any numbers common to both lists? Explain.

Activity

Use **Student Activity Sheet 1** and problems 7–11 to recreate Eratosthenes' method for extracting the prime numbers.

1	2	3	4	5	6	7	8	9	10
11	12	13	14	15	16	17	18	19	20
21	22	23	24	25	26	27	28	29	30
31	32	33	34	35	36	37	38	39	40
41	42	43	44	45	46	47	48	49	50
51	52	53	54	55	56	57	58	59	60
61	62	63	64	65	66	67	68	69	70
71	72	73	74	75	76	77	78	79	80
81	82	83	84	85	86	87	88	89	90
91	92	93	94	95	96	97	98	99	100

7. a. Circle the number 2 and put an X through all of the other multiples of 2.

b. The numbers with an X through them are not prime. Why not?

8. a. Circle 3 and put an X through all other multiples of 3.

b. Explain why you do not need to put an X through all of the multiples of 4.

c. Do you need to cross out multiples of 6? Explain why.

d. Pablo went through these steps and said, "I cannot find any number that is divisible by 12 that has not been crossed out." Is Pablo correct? Explain your answer.

e. Marisa argues that even if you extended the table to the number 1,000, all numbers in the table that are divisible by 24 would already have been crossed out. Do you agree? Explain.

Activity

9. **a.** Circle 5 and put an X through all other multiples of 5 that have not been crossed out.

   b. What is the first number you put an X through?

   c. Circle 7. Without looking at the table, name the first multiple of 7 that you will have to put an X through. How were you able to determine this number? Now cross out the other multiples of 7.

   d. Why is it unnecessary to cross out all of the multiples of 8, 9, and 10?

10. **a.** Circle 11. What multiple of 11 will you put an X through first?

    b. Circle all numbers that have not been crossed out.

    c. What numbers did you circle?

    d. In what columns do these circled numbers appear?

11. **a.** Explain why you crossed out only multiples of prime numbers.

    b. Explain why you needed to cross out multiples of primes only up to the number 11.

Prime Factors

The number 8 can be completely factored into a product of prime numbers: $8 = 2 \times 2 \times 2$.

12. **a.** Write each composite number between 2 and 10 as a product of prime numbers.

    b. Do you think it is possible to write all numbers by using only prime numbers and multiplication?

By using factor trees, you can find all of the prime factors of a number.

13. **a.** Use the factor tree method to find the prime factors of 156.

    b. Write 156 as a product of prime factors.

1	2	3	4	5	6	7	8	9	10
11	12	13	14	15	16	17	18	19	20
21	22	23	24	25	26	27	28	29	30
31	32	33	34	35	36	37	38	39	40
41	42	43	44	45	46	47	48	49	50
51	52	53	54	55	56	57	58	59	60
61	62	63	64	65	66	67	68	69	70
71	72	73	74	75	76	77	78	79	80
81	82	83	84	85	86	87	88	89	90
91	92	93	94	95	96	97	98	99	100

Name _____ Date _____ Class_____

Years, Days, Hours, Seconds

Suppose it is your birthday. People will probably ask how
old you are, and your answer will be a certain number of
years. How would you answer in terms of days, hours, and/or
seconds? Use a calculator to answer the following problems.
If the calculator's display is too small for all of the digits,
devise another way to answer the problems.

11 years old = _____ days?

I was born in 1776.
How many years old
am I?

1. How old will you be in years on your next birthday?

2. How old will you be in days on your next birthday?

3. How old will you be in hours on your next birthday?

4. How many years old will the United States be on its next
   Independence Day? (Hint: The United States became
   independent in 1776.)

5. How many hours old will the United States be on
   its next Independence Day?

I can count to
one million!

OK, I wanna
hear that!

6. How long would this take? Explain your answer,
   or show your work.

7. How many seconds old will you be on your 60th birthday?

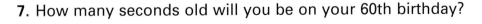

Rounding

Here is data on passenger traffic from some of the world's airports. The data is ordered alphabetically.

1. a. Make a top ten list, ordered by number of passengers.

   b. For each city on this top ten list, round the number of passengers to a whole number of millions.

City (Airport)		Total Passengers
1	Atlanta (ATL)	79,086,792
2	Amsterdam (AMS)	39,960,400
3	Bangkok (BKK)	30,175,379
4	Chicago (ORD)	69,508,672
5	Dallas/Fort Worth (DFW)	53,253,607
6	Denver (DEN)	37,505,138
7	Detroit (DTW)	32,664,620
8	Frankfurt/Main (FRA)	48,351,664
9	Hong Kong (HKG)	27,092,290
10	Houston (IAH)	34,154,574
11	Las Vegas (LAS)	36,285,932
12	London (LGW)	30,007,021
13	London/Heathrow (LHR)	63,487,136
14	Los Angeles (LAX)	54,982 838
15	Madrid (MAD)	35,854,293
16	Miami (MIA)	29,595,618
17	Minneapolis/St. Paul (MSP)	33 201,860
18	New York (JFK)	31,732,371
19	Newark (EWR)	29,431,061
20	Orlando (MCO)	27 319,223
21	Paris (CDG)	48,220,436
22	Philadelphia (PHL)	24,671,075
23	Phoenix (PHX)	37,412,165
24	Rome (FCO)	26,284,478
25	San Francisco (SFO)	29,313,271
26	Seattle (SEA)	26 755,888
27	Sydney (SYD)	25,333,508
28	Tokyo (HND)	62,876,269
29	Tokyo (NRT)	26,537,406
30	Toronto (YYZ)	24,739,312

http://www.airports.org

Key to Success

Level 3

Lesson
Three
Activities

Square and Unsquare

Square

1. a. Draw a square with the dimensions 3 cm by 3 cm.

   b. How many squares (1 cm by 1 cm) completely cover the square you just drew?

   c. Explain how squaring is related to the area of the square you drew in **a**.

2. a. Copy and complete this table filling in the area of the square with side lengths going from 1 cm through 10 cm.

Length of Side (in cm)	1	2	3	4	5	6	7	8	9	10
Area of Square (in cm²)										

   b. Is this table a ratio table? Explain why or why not.

   c. Use the grid on **Student Activity Sheet 1** to graph the information from your table. Connect all points with a smooth curve.

   d. Describe the curve of your graph. Explain what this curve tells you. Keep this graph. You will use it again in problem 7.

For problems 3–7, use centimeter graph paper.

3. a. Draw a square with the dimensions 1 cm by 1 cm.

   b. What is the area of this square?

   c. Draw a square with the dimensions $\frac{1}{2}$ cm by $\frac{1}{2}$ cm.

   d. Use your two drawings to explain that $\frac{1}{2} \times \frac{1}{2} = \frac{1}{4}$.

Now you will look at larger squares.

4. a. Draw a square with the dimensions $1\frac{1}{2}$ cm by $1\frac{1}{2}$ cm.

   b. Use this drawing to calculate the area of the square.

The number $1\frac{1}{2}$ is called a **mixed number**. It is a whole number and fraction combined.

5. **a.** Use a drawing to calculate the area of a square with side lengths of $2\frac{1}{2}$ cm.

   b. Use a drawing to calculate $3\frac{1}{2} \times 3\frac{1}{2}$.

   c. What does $(4\frac{1}{2})^2$ mean? Calculate $(4\frac{1}{2})^2$.

   d. Calculate $(5\frac{1}{2})^2$.

6. Use your results of problems 4 and 5 to add five more points to your graph of problem 2c.

Nicole uses the pattern in her answers to problem 5 to say, "There is a pattern to squaring these halves! Look, if I want to calculate $6\frac{1}{2} \times 6\frac{1}{2}$, I just calculate 6×7 and then add $\frac{1}{4}$."

7. **a.** Show how you can use your graph to see whether or not Nicole's idea makes sense.

   b. Use a drawing of a square with side lengths of $6\frac{1}{2}$ cm to show that Nicole is right. Will Nicole's idea always work? How do you know?

   c. Use Nicole's idea to calculate $9\frac{1}{2} \times 9\frac{1}{2}$.

   d. Use your graph from problem 2 to check whether or not your answer to **c** is reasonable.

   e. Use that same graph to estimate the area of a square with side lengths of 3.8 cm.

Unsquare

Cornering a Square

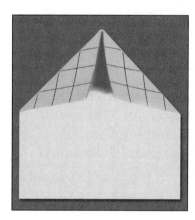

- Use **Student Activity Sheet 2**. Cut out the 8 cm by 8 cm grid. What is the area of this shape?

- Fold all four corners so that they meet in the center. What is the shape of this folded paper? What is its area? Measure the length of each side of the shape with a ruler. (Hint: You might want to look at the back of the shape.)

- Fold all four of the new corners so that they meet in the middle. Repeat this process until you have looked at a total of five shapes. Each time you fold the four corners, write down the name of the shape, the area of the shape, and the length of one of its sides.

- How does the area change each time you fold to make a new shape?

In the activity, you measured a side length of a square with an area of 32 square centimeters (cm^2). Mina did the same activity and measured the length as 5.6 cm. When Justin did the activity, he measured the length as 5.7 cm.

8. **a.** How do your measurements compare with Mina's and Justin's measurements?

   b. When Vance looked at Mina's and Justin's answers, he commented that they were close to the correct answer, but not exact. How could he tell?

Not So Square

The floor of Nathan's room is $2\frac{1}{2}$ m by $4\frac{1}{2}$ m. His room will be redecorated, and the floor will be redone. In order to estimate the cost of the new floor covering, Nathan estimates the area of the floor to be about $8\frac{1}{4}$ m².

9. a. How did Nathan arrive at his answer?

   b. Show that this answer cannot be right.

   c. On graph paper, make a scale drawing of the floor of Nathan's room. Use the scale drawing to calculate the area of the floor.

During the fall, Nathan earns extra money working at the apple orchard. In one hour, he fills $3\frac{1}{2}$ bushels of apples. How many bushels will he fill after working $6\frac{1}{2}$ hours?

A solution to this problem involves calculating $3\frac{1}{2} \times 6\frac{1}{2}$. Although bushels of apples and hours are involved, you can use the **area model** to make a calculation. In this case, the area is $3\frac{1}{2} \times 6\frac{1}{2}$, and the rectangle is $3\frac{1}{2}$ by $6\frac{1}{2}$.

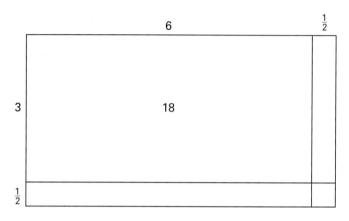

10. **a.** Copy the area model above and use it to find the number of bushels of apples Nathan will fill after working for $6\frac{1}{2}$ hours.

   b. Use the area model to calculate $3\frac{1}{2} \times 4\frac{1}{2}$.

   c. Use the area model to calculate $5\frac{1}{2} \times 11\frac{1}{2}$.

Name _____

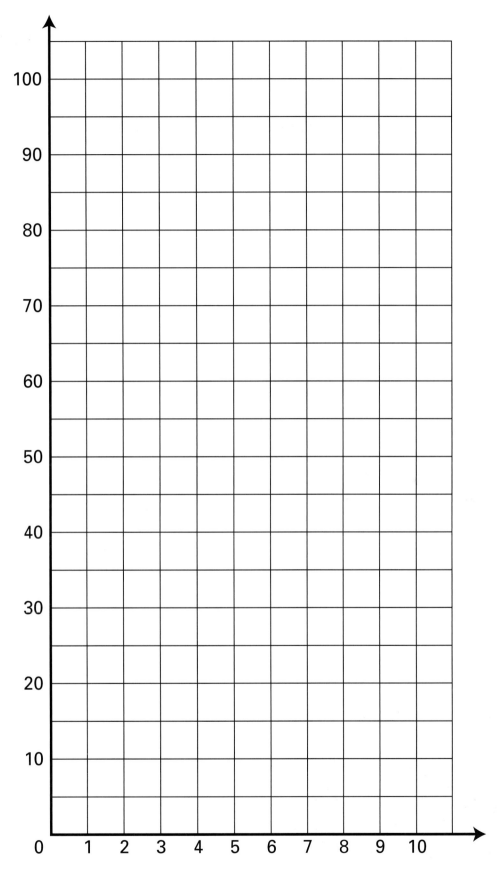

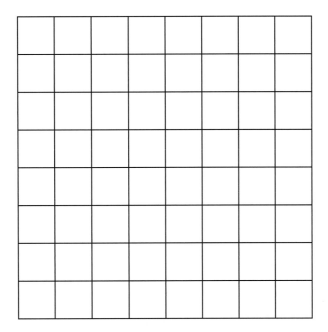

Squares (page 1)

5^2 is a shorter notation for 5×5.

Somebody wrote this (we are not telling who!):

$13^2 = 13 \times 13$ $24^2 = 24 \times 24$

      $= 109$ $= 416$

1. Use your calculator to show that the two answers are wrong. What did this student do?

This large square consists of 13 small squares across by 13 small squares down.

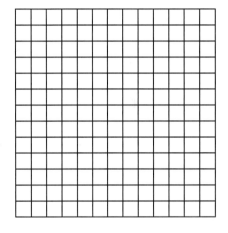

   2. **a.** Shade the parts of the large square that represent 10×10 and 3×3.

      b. If you think $13^2 = (10 \times 10) + (3 \times 3)$, you are really missing two parts. Write the number of small squares in those two parts.

      c. Add the numbers of small squares in the four parts. Is this equal to 13^2?

To find 24^2, you can think of a large square that consists of 24 times 24 small squares. You do not have to draw the small squares. You can imagine that they are there and write the dimensions of the four parts along outer edge. The drawing does not need to be to scale.

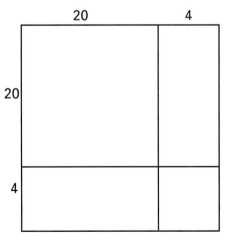

   3. **a.** Write the number of small squares that would be in each of the four parts if they were all drawn.

      b. What is the answer to $24^2 =$ _____?

Squares (page 2)

4. **a.** Find the area of each of the four parts.

   b. What is the answer to 15^2?

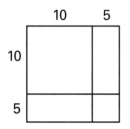

5. **a.** Find the area of each of the four parts.

   b. What is the answer to 25^2?

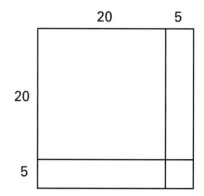

6. Find the answer to 35^2.

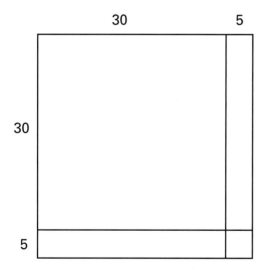

7. Find the answer to 45^2.

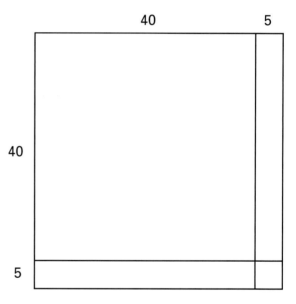

8. Find 55^2 and 65^2.

9. What pattern do you notice? How would you use this pattern to calculate 95^2?

Key to Success

BRITANNICA
Mathematics
in
Context

Level 3

Lesson
Four
Activities

Are People Getting Taller?

The Turn of the Century:
The Pearson and Lee Investigation

"Have you ever slept in a really old bed and noticed it was a lot smaller than your bed?"

Other people have noticed this too. Around 1900, statisticians Karl Pearson and Alice Lee decided to collect data that would help them determine whether or not children grow to be taller than their parents. They asked people to measure the height of each member of their family over the age of 18.

  1. a. Why did everyone have to be over 18 years old for the survey?

  b. Reflect Why do you think it might be important to see if children grow taller than their parents?

The Pearson and Lee Data

The heights, in inches, of 1,064 pairs of fathers and sons from the Pearson and Lee data are listed in **Appendix A** at the end of this lesson. These data were reconstructed from Pearson and Lee's study.

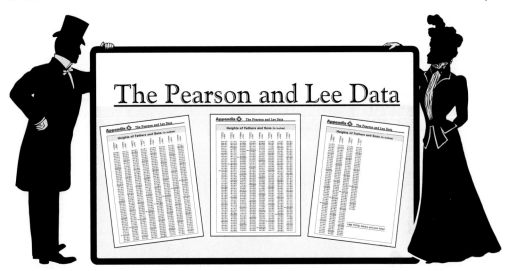

If you need to work with a long list of numbers, it helps to explore the data first.

2. From the data set in **Appendix A**, find the following:

    a. an example of a son who was at least 6 inches taller than his father

    b. an example of a father and son with the same height

    c. an example of a son who was shorter than his father

    d. an example of a son who was at least 6 inches shorter than his father

3. a. Which one of the examples in problem 2 was easy to find? Why?

    b. Which was the most difficult?

By studying the data, Pearson and Lee concluded that sons grow to be taller than their fathers.

4. **Reflect** Describe what you think Pearson and Lee did with the data in order to reach their conclusion.

The Pearson and Lee Sample

Pearson and Lee were convinced that they had enough data.

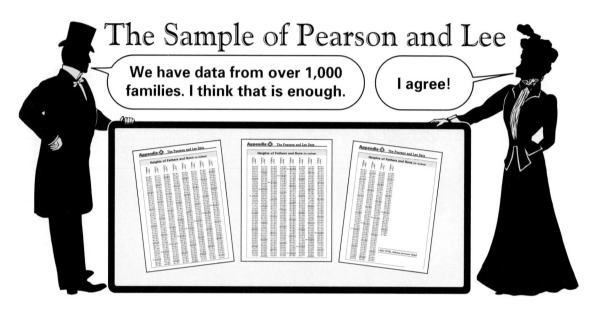

5. How could this be when they knew that there were many fathers and sons for whom they had no data?

The group of families that Pearson and Lee studied is called a **sample**. A sample is a group taken from the whole population.

Sampling

To make valid conclusions about the whole population, the person gathering the data must choose a sample in a proper way. Conclusions from the sample about the characteristic they are studying, such as height, eye color, or favorite food, must also be true for the whole population. If the process of sampling is not carefully done, then the results are unreliable.

Pearson and Lee collected their data in England in 1903 by asking college students to measure the heights of their own family members and of people in other families they knew.

6. Do you think the Pearson and Lee sample was chosen in a proper way? Do you think the conclusions are valid for everyone in England at that time?

Activity

You and your classmates can collect some current data to see how heights in families might be related today.

Find the heights of some mother-daughter pairs. Remember that the daughters should be at least 18 years old. Then gather all of the data from your classmates.

Use your data on mother-daughter pairs for the following problems.

• Make a list of the heights of the mother-daughter pairs collected by your classmates. Organize your data like the list in **Appendix A**.

• Make some statements about the data you collected.

Scatter Plots

Graphs and Tables

Graphs and tables help you see patterns and trends in long lists of data.

Pearson and Lee wanted to make a graph that would help them understand more about the relationship between the heights of fathers and sons.

Shown here are the heights of five pairs of fathers and sons, taken from the Pearson and Lee data.

	Fathers' Heights (in inches)	Sons' Heights (in inches)
A	66.8	68.4
B	68.5	69.4
C	65.6	67.5
D	70.0	67.8
E	67.5	67.5

You can plot the heights of each father-son pair with a point on the grid on **Student Activity Sheet 1**.

The heights of all of the fathers and sons range from 58 to 80 inches.

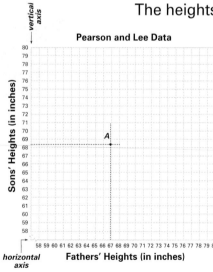

The scale along the bottom of the graph is called the **horizontal axis**. Another scale is marked off on a line that goes up and down on the paper. This is called the **vertical axis**.

The graph shows the location of point *A*, which corresponds to the father-son pair *A* at (66.8, 68.4).

7. **a.** Put this point on the grid on **Student Activity Sheet 1**. Explain how you plotted this point.

   b. Plot points *B, C, D,* and *E* on the grid on **Student Activity Sheet 1**.

   c. What statement can you make about the heights of fathers and sons from the points you plotted?

If you plot all 1,064 pairs of data that are in **Appendix A**, on the grid on **Student Activity Sheet 1**, you would get the diagram below. It is called a **scatter plot**. The points are "scattered" across the diagram. By making a scatter plot, you create a picture of your data.

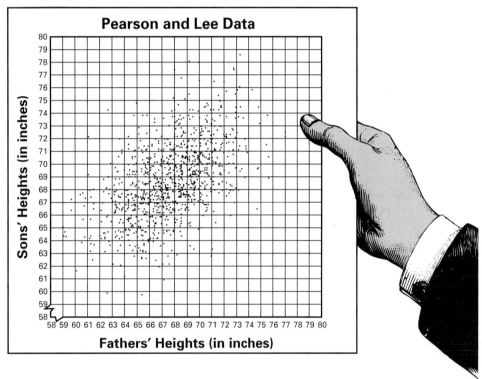

8. The numbers along the axes of the scatter plot start with 58, not 0. Why is this?

Use the copy of the scatter plot on **Student Activity Sheet 2** for problem 9.

9. **a.** Circle the point that represents the tallest father. How tall is he? How tall is his son? Is he the tallest son?

   b. Circle the point that represents the shortest father. How tall is he? Is he taller than his son? How does the height of his son compare to the heights of the other sons?

Heights of Fathers and Sons (in inches)

Fathers	Sons	Fathers	Sons	Fathers	Sons	Fathers	Sons	Fathers	Sons	Fathers	Sons	Fathers	Sons	Fathers	Sons
66.8	68.4	64.5	71.1	69.4	69.4	66.5	68.1	69.5	68.0	66.5	73.4	68.3	69.1	74.4	69.6
68.5	69.4	66.2	70.3	69.2	69.5	63.8	71.8	65.8	64.9	68.9	70.9	67.4	68.0	70.1	67.7
65.6	67.5	66.0	70.4	65.4	65.2	68.2	69.4	69.7	72.5	69.8	67.2	65.0	69.2	66.9	68.0
70.0	67.8	69.3	67.3	66.7	68.6	65.3	65.1	68.5	67.5	68.0	71.1	70.3	66.9	65.6	67.4
68.7	71.4	67.4	68.0	70.3	69.9	65.4	59.7	68.5	66.2	69.9	70.4	66.9	63.8	70.0	68.3
67.5	67.5	73.0	71.3	64.0	62.7	71.6	69.2	66.8	67.4	69.5	69.3	63.5	67.2	68.8	70.4
61.2	64.5	68.5	67.7	68.4	64.8	66.6	68.5	65.9	73.6	70.3	74.2	70.8	68.8	72.3	66.1
68.5	76.4	65.9	69.6	67.2	67.7	66.9	70.9	70.5	73.1	63.4	67.9	65.6	70.3	70.0	67.3
66.5	68.0	71.1	71.1	72.5	72.5	67.4	70.4	63.5	68.8	59.6	64.9	67.8	73.9	67.9	65.0
65.9	67.8	69.5	68.2	66.7	64.4	66.0	68.5	61.0	67.8	68.5	72.7	61.1	66.8	66.8	67.6
65.0	66.9	68.7	70.0	67.4	67.4	65.9	72.3	69.5	68.0	65.4	65.3	70.0	71.3	65.5	62.9
68.1	69.9	72.0	69.9	65.7	66.3	71.6	74.3	70.0	72.7	66.5	65.5	64.5	64.6	70.6	70.3
68.0	70.8	69.7	68.8	67.7	71.0	68.8	66.6	69.5	67.6	70.7	70.0	67.5	67.7	66.8	66.3
66.5	67.0	69.5	69.8	65.0	66.5	72.5	70.0	69.2	65.6	67.2	73.4	70.6	69.2	64.4	64.7
68.4	73.0	66.4	65.8	61.1	66.3	68.5	68.0	66.7	67.8	65.7	68.4	72.0	73.5	68.0	69.8
68.3	72.8	71.5	72.7	66.7	66.7	67.9	71.0	69.8	69.1	66.7	68.8	70.5	70.9	68.6	69.3
62.9	66.1	65.6	67.0	65.0	66.6	64.8	65.3	62.8	66.0	69.0	69.0	64.6	63.9	67.0	68.2
64.0	71.0	68.3	68.1	63.7	67.6	67.3	65.0	66.0	70.2	65.8	67.7	70.3	71.8	69.8	73.9
61.7	62.8	67.0	70.0	66.2	67.8	66.2	68.7	70.5	69.9	69.3	73.3	67.0	72.0	62.4	65.7
69.1	67.3	69.0	71.4	67.9	71.3	66.5	69.6	67.3	70.2	76.6	72.3	64.1	64.9	71.3	70.4
70.0	71.5	68.0	67.0	67.2	60.9	69.5	71.7	67.0	70.2	65.6	67.1	65.8	63.4	63.7	65.6
71.0	70.9	69.2	74.0	70.4	74.3	69.4	68.5	66.3	67.6	68.8	72.3	70.0	70.8	62.7	64.7
68.0	67.8	69.4	71.8	67.3	65.7	70.0	71.8	67.1	66.3	65.5	67.3	63.9	64.9	63.2	67.4
66.0	64.3	64.9	70.9	66.3	69.7	68.5	71.5	71.0	68.4	67.5	68.0	65.0	67.5	67.7	68.2
70.6	72.4	61.8	63.9	64.4	69.2	71.7	69.7	68.0	67.1	67.1	68.0	65.3	65.3	66.0	69.3
64.7	66.8	67.6	71.4	60.1	66.5	70.9	68.7	69.2	69.5	69.2	70.3	69.5	68.5	70.9	63.6
67.9	71.1	63.7	65.0	66.6	65.5	67.4	70.0	65.5	65.0	72.2	67.8	66.5	67.0	68.7	70.4
67.3	71.1	68.3	71.3	66.6	67.7	67.3	67.1	65.7	63.9	65.7	64.9	68.4	67.6	65.3	63.7
70.3	68.5	65.3	63.9	70.7	70.9	64.5	65.8	68.4	73.6	64.8	65.4	66.9	68.3	69.7	69.2
65.6	63.5	68.5	68.3	64.5	71.4	69.5	63.6	68.0	77.4	64.5	66.7	65.0	66.7	67.6	67.4
65.3	67.5	68.9	71.2	69.6	71.8	69.4	70.0	67.3	68.6	68.2	67.0	68.3	67.9	70.2	70.7
64.6	69.5	68.4	67.8	65.3	63.4	68.6	70.5	65.4	67.5	62.5	67.1	65.5	71.0	69.8	70.3
70.7	70.3	67.3	68.3	67.6	66.9	67.2	66.7	65.8	66.4	69.5	66.9	67.2	70.0	63.4	67.7
67.3	67.7	67.6	70.5	71.5	69.8	69.2	69.6	64.0	68.6	67.1	68.8	70.1	68.6	65.4	71.7
67.9	67.2	68.0	69.7	66.6	65.6	69.5	68.6	71.4	68.4	75.1	71.4	68.0	66.6	63.5	66.5
68.4	68.7	66.2	67.2	65.8	62.9	71.0	66.4	69.3	68.8	66.4	67.3	66.9	68.0	60.1	67.3
69.5	68.2	70.9	71.4	69.9	69.3	69.5	70.8	65.1	69.4	63.4	68.4	67.7	68.9	70.8	74.0
72.2	70.0	66.2	70.3	69.1	68.4	66.5	64.7	69.3	65.4	65.2	66.8	65.6	65.0	67.4	69.2
66.4	69.2	67.3	69.7	68.9	70.5	66.2	67.3	69.1	67.6	66.9	66.6	66.6	65.9	65.3	65.7
72.5	71.0	70.0	72.1	65.8	71.1	68.9	68.5	70.1	72.6	64.7	70.5	66.4	66.4	63.9	65.8
66.7	68.3	68.1	69.8	67.3	71.7	66.6	71.8	71.3	70.0	65.0	65.5	71.3	72.5	68.0	68.8
68.3	73.3	69.5	70.5	67.7	70.6	64.6	69.2	63.6	64.6	67.9	66.5	68.1	65.6	68.5	65.7
68.6	71.3	69.5	72.3	64.7	67.7	70.5	66.5	68.5	69.8	65.8	68.5	68.5	69.5	60.9	64.1
65.7	66.6	61.4	69.2	66.5	65.4	70.6	71.2	70.3	70.6	62.7	64.5	63.5	66.9	70.9	73.3
70.4	73.3	72.4	68.3	68.7	67.7	66.3	69.5	67.3	67.0	71.6	72.8	67.6	70.6	67.4	66.8
68.8	70.4	67.6	72.8	72.1	70.5	64.0	66.5	70.5	69.7	71.5	73.6	65.9	70.4	70.7	69.1
65.9	69.3	64.9	73.6	70.0	72.3	64.1	65.6	66.1	66.0	71.5	70.0	68.5	68.0	68.1	67.2
70.6	71.1	68.6	68.8	73.1	74.3	63.2	70.0	63.5	67.9	69.6	70.8	69.1	75.2	67.5	68.2
67.8	73.5	66.5	66.7	70.4	68.3	64.9	67.3	65.5	68.0	70.6	66.9	72.9	71.0	65.6	66.4
71.2	71.0	63.5	66.3	68.5	70.2	67.8	67.8	65.5	67.0	69.5	67.8	71.6	71.2	67.9	74.9
72.7	77.5	65.6	73.6	69.5	69.2	64.9	64.8	69.3	69.3	61.8	66.6	69.0	69.1	67.2	70.9
66.7	64.4	65.8	71.0	71.6	71.4	67.9	69.5	68.0	66.5	65.7	67.9	72.0	72.2	70.7	70.4
65.6	64.3	73.4	68.9	67.2	66.2	63.7	70.5	65.9	66.3	71.9	72.0	63.7	68.5	71.4	75.1
67.7	68.9	66.9	66.0	69.2	70.5	68.4	69.0	70.4	66.9	74.5	74.2	71.1	68.0	73.3	73.4

(Row-count markers shown along the columns: 50, 100, 150, 200, 250, 300, 350, 400)

Appendix A — Pearson and Lee's Data

Heights of Fathers and Sons (in inches)

Fathers–Sons	Fathers–Sons	Fathers–Sons	Fathers–Sons	Fathers–Sons	Fathers–Sons	Fathers–Sons	Fathers–Sons
69.8–70.6	67.1–70.8	66.7–67.6	72.4–72.6	65.6–68.6	67.4–66.6	71.0–72.2	69.8–65.1
69.6–70.2	67.5–71.9	64.8–65.4	67.6–69.5	66.3–68.0	69.4–74.0	69.6–69.2	63.5–64.5
69.0–70.4	69.5–70.9	66.1–64.3	70.6–71.7	69.0–70.3	70.5–66.7	68.1–70.7	70.3–68.1
66.4–64.4	66.0–67.4	68.0–68.6	65.1–74.5	70.8–71.8	71.8–72.2	66.3–71.4	68.6–72.1
69.0–71.7	71.0–69.4	64.8–67.4	68.5–71.4	66.4–68.2	70.4–66.4	69.9–70.5	66.7–71.1
65.6–63.4	65.3–66.6	63.6–68.0	70.2–67.2	61.4–72.0	69.5–67.3	70.5–70.0	66.8–64.8
63.0–64.2	69.1–71.7	70.5–69.3	74.5–69.7	68.1–72.6	64.5–67.0	68.2–69.7	68.2–65.8
63.0–69.0	68.6–70.6	72.9–73.5	65.1–64.9	70.9–69.8	66.3–66.0	69.9–78.0	68.5–69.8
73.5–71.1	66.2–70.4	65.5–67.4	64.8–63.5	65.0–63.8	68.6–68.1	67.4–66.0	67.3–65.4
68.0–68.3	69.1–71.8	69.4–68.4	61.0–65.8	68.7–70.1	70.2–67.0	67.6–69.3	73.5–71.3
72.0–72.0	64.6–65.0	66.4–69.8	67.1–66.8	68.0–69.2	63.9–63.9	67.0–67.5	66.1–68.9
65.5–65.8	63.7–69.4	67.9–66.6	64.0–66.6	60.8–67.7	66.0–67.4	66.7–68.9	69.1–73.6
68.0–70.9	64.3–67.5	65.8–69.0	71.5–74.7	69.6–70.9	69.6–68.6	66.4–68.3	67.5–67.1
69.6–69.4	68.6–69.2	63.5–66.9	67.2–67.4	67.4–66.6	70.3–68.7	65.1–67.6	68.2–67.0
66.9–68.9	65.7–67.8	68.7–72.3	70.4–71.4	64.0–67.8	72.9–68.0	66.5–70.1	64.1–66.7
70.9–70.0	69.6–68.3	64.5–66.8	67.2–66.3	69.0–71.2	59.5–64.6	65.8–69.7	65.6–62.5
64.7–69.0	68.8–67.5	68.0–68.6	70.6–67.1	69.1–67.1	62.3–64.6	69.1–66.5	69.2–63.8
75.3–70.5	64.9–63.1	70.4–72.7	63.1–68.1	65.3–68.7	68.5–65.6	72.8–77.4	70.0–68.3
67.5–65.8	68.0–71.2	68.0–66.4	65.1–67.6	73.3–78.6	70.8–71.6	63.3–67.2	70.9–70.2
73.0–75.7	65.9–68.5	72.0–76.5	68.5–69.7	69.7–69.9	73.4–71.8	66.7–66.3	69.7–69.5
66.0–69.2	69.2–69.1	63.3–61.4	68.6–66.9	62.6–68.8	67.0–65.5	71.8–69.5	72.0–71.9
62.6–67.9	75.2–73.6	67.7–66.3	68.3–66.5	72.5–68.0	68.1–68.3	70.8–73.0	70.5–74.5
68.7–68.3	65.3–68.2	61.6–64.6	66.4–64.8	65.6–67.7	63.9–67.5	67.1–62.5	68.8–67.7
71.4–67.7	74.6–73.0	67.0–68.5	69.4–69.2	64.3–65.0	69.6–70.3	69.3–68.7	69.4–70.2
72.7–73.4	64.7–65.5	66.3–71.3	67.1–67.7	68.4–69.6	66.8–67.0	63.9–62.4	67.1–69.3
67.2–67.5	62.4–66.5	65.3–72.7	69.5–72.7	65.0–66.8	72.3–68.0	69.9–69.3	66.3–66.1
69.4–69.3	69.6–68.2	71.6–74.2	71.5–69.2	60.5–62.0	66.7–68.6	66.7–72.5	70.4–66.9
67.7–69.6	70.0–70.1	66.1–65.6	68.6–68.0	71.4–69.8	69.6–69.3	69.8–68.1	64.3–66.9
69.0–69.5	63.0–67.8	61.8–68.1	61.5–64.4	67.7–69.3	69.0–66.7	68.6–69.4	68.4–68.0
64.2–69.5	64.8–70.4	64.7–67.7	68.4–69.8	66.3–69.8	68.1–68.5	65.0–71.0	67.7–71.4
64.5–64.3	66.1–65.3	67.4–64.9	68.5–68.9	65.3–71.2	66.5–70.7	70.8–63.1	68.5–69.0
66.7–67.0	66.7–67.3	65.4–67.0	70.4–66.6	65.2–64.5	64.8–69.4	68.0–65.8	67.5–71.8
66.1–69.9	71.8–70.8	69.9–70.2	67.4–65.0	64.7–65.9	68.3–68.5	70.0–67.1	65.0–69.0
65.1–66.0	64.8–68.6	67.7–69.7	70.1–72.4	68.0–69.1	71.2–70.1	69.4–71.3	66.8–62.3
69.3–68.5	72.0–75.4	66.4–66.6	67.5–67.7	68.4–67.5	66.8–68.7	68.3–74.4	68.0–71.4
67.7–67.1	70.0–70.7	67.9–67.1	72.3–72.2	65.4–63.5	68.4–65.3	70.5–68.4	70.7–70.7
62.6–59.9	67.6–66.5	67.3–67.2	65.2–65.2	69.3–69.7	67.7–66.7	69.7–71.3	68.1–73.1
63.3–62.5	65.7–67.3	67.0–70.3	66.1–66.3	70.2–69.4	67.9–64.9	68.5–66.6	65.1–70.0
68.7–72.4	68.0–72.0	67.7–71.6	69.9–70.2	69.2–68.2	71.2–65.6	64.7–68.4	70.7–72.4
63.8–68.8	71.4–74.0	68.7–67.7	66.4–64.2	71.7–68.0	65.7–69.2	69.3–69.9	65.8–69.4
65.8–69.3	69.1–67.7	68.2–71.3	66.8–70.9	68.8–68.1	63.4–66.3	65.9–65.7	66.8–66.7
70.5–67.6	68.2–73.2	63.8–67.0	66.5–65.0	63.8–64.4	68.9–67.9	72.0–68.6	69.6–69.3
67.8–68.8	59.0–65.1	71.7–71.5	64.0–64.5	67.3–71.5	70.9–71.8	66.6–62.8	69.8–70.0
65.5–64.7	69.7–69.0	72.5–71.6	67.6–65.0	66.9–68.1	67.1–68.1	66.8–69.5	66.5–65.3
64.5–67.3	63.5–64.9	68.7–73.4	70.1–72.1	65.3–72.2	72.7–68.2	70.0–67.5	69.4–67.7
63.5–66.4	72.2–69.3	67.3–68.3	72.3–68.0	69.6–69.4	70.1–70.8	75.3–68.9	67.0–66.0
69.3–71.3	66.7–67.0	62.4–64.4	69.2–70.2	72.2–71.6	66.0–67.0	68.8–74.8	73.0–69.5
70.8–72.9	66.2–66.0	70.8–72.1	68.3–68.1	66.2–64.4	67.0–67.9	69.8–69.9	71.1–73.2
69.7–70.8	61.6–64.0	68.7–68.4	66.6–68.3	67.8–68.6	70.4–69.3	68.7–70.5	64.5–67.2
72.0–71.5	64.8–68.5	68.9–66.7	68.6–70.4	66.5–68.9	61.2–67.4	64.5–69.0	72.8–75.5
66.6–69.0	64.7–66.1	66.8–71.5	67.1–67.5	69.8–70.4	70.3–69.7	68.5–67.7	70.2–72.4
68.3–70.6	65.0–70.5	63.8–67.5	72.7–73.8	72.5–71.0	68.9–70.5	69.2–69.2	68.5–73.3
70.0–76.6	64.7–65.3	67.8–70.0	69.3–69.0	68.5–69.0	71.0–69.0	72.0–68.1	66.0–71.3
71.0–74.0	64.4–66.6	72.0–67.6	67.8–63.5	69.1–65.5	66.8–71.7	64.5–65.7	72.5–70.7

(Row markers along the columns: 450, 500, 550, 600, 650, 700, 750, 800, 850)

Heights of Fathers and Sons (in inches)

Fathers / Sons	Fathers / Sons	Fathers / Sons	Fathers / Sons
65.4–67.0	66.1–67.7	72.7–75.2	64.9–66.5
73.6–70.8	71.2–71.6	64.5–65.9	62.7–64.4
68.0–69.8	68.7–71.7	69.3–67.2	66.0–64.2
71.0–70.1	66.0–66.9	72.2–70.9	72.6–67.1
62.9–69.0	69.1–67.1	67.2–64.8	66.6–69.3
72.7–74.2	72.7–69.7	67.2–64.0	67.2–67.3
64.4–67.7	70.0–69.3	65.8–69.8	64.3–66.4
68.3–68.3	67.6–69.9	63.8–66.6	67.4–71.3
68.2–72.0	65.4–69.4	66.5–69.1	67.4–68.1
67.4–68.1	68.4–68.4	61.6–67.5	72.3–68.4
67.7–70.5	66.5–70.5	68.8–66.9	67.0–68.6
63.7–66.7	64.6–65.9	64.5–67.7	68.5–65.5
67.7–64.7	65.8–67.0	67.5–68.4	70.3–71.5
67.7–70.6	68.7–67.7	72.7–71.9	63.2–65.7
67.5–70.1	65.5–69.6	68.4–71.2	68.9–67.7
65.8–66.2	62.9–74.0	67.5–69.2	67.8–66.3
70.9–71.5	65.6–67.4	69.8–69.4	67.4–65.5
64.5–72.0	62.9–64.9	65.7–64.0	66.7–66.5
68.5–72.0	66.5–73.1	70.4–70.9	68.0–68.5
62.7–63.4	68.0–72.2	64.9–66.9	59.3–64.3
67.0–71.0	71.3–70.4	66.9–66.3	65.0–68.3
69.5–68.7	63.7–69.4	69.9–71.3	70.3–68.2
64.3–68.0	67.6–70.3	66.0–67.1	71.5–69.3
64.5–65.1	71.5–71.0	68.6–68.2 *(1,050)*	68.4–67.5
67.5–63.1	69.8–70.6	61.6–65.8	65.5–63.0
70.1–65.2	62.6–64.8	76.6–72.0	66.4–65.7
64.8–69.2	70.8–67.9	69.2–78.1	70.6–74.3
67.3–68.4	69.2–67.5 *(1,000)*	72.8–72.3	66.1–67.0
69.4–70.6	69.9–73.4	70.1–70.0	67.2–66.7
70.8–68.2	70.3–69.5	67.7–69.0	69.3–72.2
64.5–69.9	64.3–65.1	63.6–66.8	63.6–66.7
74.0–75.5	66.7–70.1 *(950)*	67.0–69.8	66.3–67.7
71.0–68.7	66.3–67.9	68.0–73.5	65.7–70.0
66.0–65.4	64.9–69.9	65.0–67.7	67.6–67.5
71.4–68.5	67.3–68.2	65.6–64.6	68.8–66.5
66.4–66.6 *(900)*	69.3–69.0	68.5–65.9	67.3–68.8
62.8–68.2	70.9–70.8	70.5–73.2	71.7–68.7
63.7–63.5	62.8–68.2	68.0–74.0	67.1–68.0
68.9–69.9	69.3–68.2	67.9–68.0	
67.5–70.0	69.4–73.5	71.1–72.8	
69.5–69.4	69.6–67.3	65.5–69.4	
65.7–71.3	65.7–68.0	64.8–66.5	
65.6–70.8	63.1–63.9	61.6–63.4	
64.0–70.8	61.8–67.0	65.7–68.5	
68.2–63.2	68.9–70.8	71.6–74.3	
70.4–71.5	65.1–68.4	68.7–67.7	
63.5–69.7	67.0–68.5	71.2–76.5	
66.9–67.3	64.4–68.0	70.5–69.5	
67.4–68.2	70.1–72.8	70.5–73.6	
70.4–70.4	70.2–66.1	73.2–69.6	
67.7–70.0	66.0–70.1	69.0–71.7	
61.5–68.0	69.8–70.4	68.5–69.4	
68.0–65.9	66.1–68.7	69.4–69.3	
69.3–71.0	69.3–69.1	68.3–67.5	

1,064 TOTAL fathers and sons listed

Pearson and Lee Data

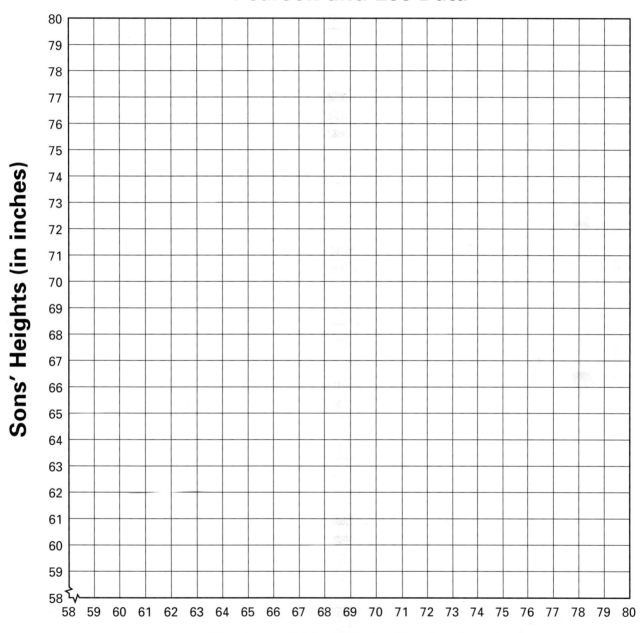

Sons' Heights (in inches)

Fathers' Heights (in inches)

BRITANNICA

Mathematics
in
Context

Key to Success

Pearson and Lee Data

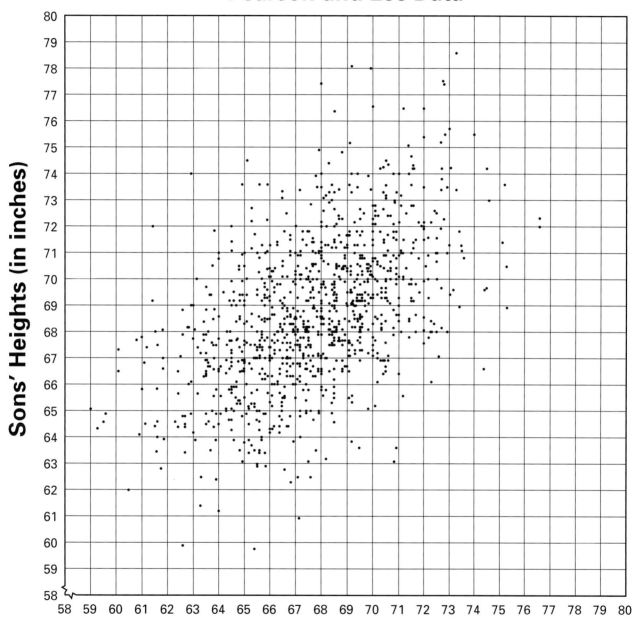

Sons' Heights (in inches)

Fathers' Heights (in inches)

1. A school needs to purchase 513 new computers. If each computer costs $3,470, what is the total cost of these new computers? Use your calculator to solve this problem.

DO NOT use your calculator to solve the following problems. Instead, use your answer from problem 1 as a starting point to calculate the new results.

2. A ticket to the circus costs $5.13. If 347 people attended the circus, what is the total ticket revenue?

3. Every year, a ferryboat sails 3,470 times from the mainland to the island of Olku. The maximum number of passengers allowed on the ferry is 5,130. What is the maximum number of people that the boat can carry to the island each year?

4. Pierre pays $34.70 for one kilogram of specialty mushrooms. What would he pay for 5.13 kilograms of mushrooms?

5. Mr. Flores is making some of the costumes for the school play. He needs 51.3 yards of fabric, and the fabric costs $3.47 a yard. What is the total cost for the fabric?

Decimal Point (page 2)

Louis used a calculator for his homework. Three minutes before handing in his work the next day, he notices that none of his answers has a decimal point. It is too late to re-do the work, so he decides to do each problem mentally. Do you think he can do this in two minutes?

How long does it take you? Time yourself and see how many you complete.

1. a. $6.25 \times 1.3 = 8125$

b. $25.1 \times 4.17 = 104667$

c. $2.125 \times 421.6 = 8959$

d. $0.85 \times 1.5 = 1275$

2. a. $384.75 \div 135 = 285$

b. $384.75 \div 13.5 = 285$

c. $384.75 \div 1.35 = 285$

d. $269.61 \div 28.5 = 946$

Key to Success

BRITANNICA

Mathematics
in
Context

Level 3

Lesson
Five
Activities

Stem-and-Leaf Plots and Histograms

Stem-and-Leaf Plots

Theodore Roosevelt was the youngest person to become president of the United States. He was 42 at his inauguration. John F. Kennedy was 43, making him the second youngest.

Theodore Roosevelt

John F. Kennedy

1. **a.** Is it possible for a 40-year-old to be president of the United States?

   b. **Reflect** How old do you think a president of the United States should be?

Pages 51 and 52 show when all of the presidents of the United States were born, when they were inaugurated as president, and when they died.

2. Who was the oldest person ever to become president of the United States?

Name	Born	Inaugurated	at Age	Died	at Age
George Washington	Feb. 22, 1732	1789	57	Dec. 14, 1799	67
John Adams	Oct. 30, 1735	1797	61	Jul. 4, 1826	90
Thomas Jefferson	Apr. 13, 1743	1801	57	Jul. 4, 1826	83
James Madison	Mar. 16, 1751	1809	57	Jun. 28, 1836	85
James Monroe	Apr. 28, 1758	1817	58	Jul. 4, 1831	73
John Q. Adams	Jul. 11, 1767	1825	57	Feb. 23, 1848	80
Andrew Jackson	Mar. 15, 1767	1829	61	Jun. 8, 1845	78
Martin Van Buren	Dec. 5, 1782	1837	54	Jul. 24, 1862	79
William H. Harrison	Feb. 9, 1773	1841	68	Apr. 4, 1841	68
John Tyler	Mar. 29, 1790	1841	51	Jan. 18, 1862	71
James K. Polk	Nov. 2, 1795	1845	49	Jun. 15, 1849	53
Zachary Taylor	Nov. 24, 1784	1849	64	Jul. 9, 1850	65
Millard Fillmore	Jan. 7, 1800	1850	50	Mar. 8, 1874	74
Franklin Pierce	Nov. 23, 1804	1853	48	Oct. 8, 1869	64
James Buchanan	Apr. 23, 1791	1857	65	Jun. 1, 1868	77
Abraham Lincoln	Feb. 12, 1809	1861	52	Apr. 15, 1865	56
Andrew Johnson	Dec. 29, 1808	1865	56	Jul. 31, 1875	66
Ulysses S. Grant	Apr. 27, 1822	1869	46	Jul. 23, 1885	63
Rutherford B. Hayes	Oct. 4, 1822	1877	54	Jan. 17, 1893	70
James A. Garfield	Nov. 19, 1831	1881	49	Sep. 19, 1881	49
Chester A. Arthur	Oct. 5, 1829	1881	51	Nov. 18, 1886	57
Grover Cleveland	Mar. 18, 1837	1885	47	Jun. 24, 1908	71
Benjamin Harrison	Aug. 20, 1833	1889	55	Mar. 13, 1901	67
Grover Cleveland	Mar. 18, 1837	1893	55	Jun. 24, 1908	71
William McKinley	Jan. 29, 1843	1897	54	Sep. 14, 1901	58

Lesson Five Activities

	Name	Born	Inaugurated	at Age	Died	at Age
	Theodore Roosevelt	Oct. 27, 1858	1901	42	Jan. 6, 1919	60
	William H. Taft	Sep. 15, 1857	1909	51	Mar. 8, 1930	72
	Woodrow Wilson	Dec. 28, 1856	1913	56	Feb. 3, 1924	67
	Warren G. Harding	Nov. 2, 1865	1921	55	Aug. 2, 1923	57
	Calvin Coolidge	Jul. 4, 1872	1923	51	Jan. 5, 1933	60
	Herbert C. Hoover	Aug. 10, 1874	1929	54	Oct. 20, 1964	90
	Franklin D. Roosevelt	Jan. 30, 1882	1933	51	Apr.12, 1945	63
	Harry S. Truman	May 8, 1884	1945	60	Dec. 26, 1972	88
	Dwight D. Eisenhower	Oct. 14, 1890	1953	62	Mar. 28, 1969	78
	John F. Kennedy	May 29, 1917	1961	43	Nov. 22, 1963	46
	Lyndon B. Johnson	Aug. 27, 1908	1963	55	Jan. 22, 1973	64
	Richard M. Nixon*	Jan. 9, 1913	1969	56	Apr. 22, 1994	81
	Gerald R. Ford	Jul. 14, 1913	1974	61		
	James E. Carter	Oct. 1, 1924	1977	52		
	Ronald Reagan	Feb. 6, 1911	1981	69	Jun. 5, 2004	93
	George Bush	Jun. 12, 1924	1989	64		
	William J. Clinton	Aug. 19, 1946	1993	46		
	George W. Bush	Jul. 6, 1946	2001	54		

*Resigned Aug. 9, 1974

Most of the presidents were from 50 to 54 years old at the time of inauguration.

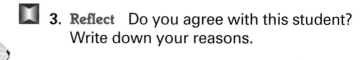

3. **Reflect** Do you agree with this student? Write down your reasons.

It is possible to organize the numbers into a new list or a diagram that makes it easier to see the distribution of the ages of the presidents at inauguration. This can be done in several ways.

4. **a.** Organize the numbers into a new list or a diagram that makes it easier to see the distribution of the ages of the presidents at inauguration.

   b. Write some conclusions that you can draw from the list or diagram that you made for part **a**.

Sarah made a **dot plot** of the presidents' ages at the time of their inauguration.

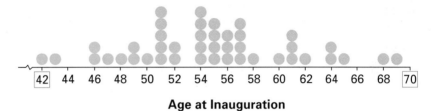

Age at Inauguration

5. **a.** What information is easier to see in this graph than in the list on pages 51 and 52?

   b. What information is missing?

6. Write at least three conclusions that you can draw from Sarah's dot plot. Write them in sentences beginning, for example:

   • Most presidents were about _____ at the time of their inauguration.

   • Very few presidents _____ .

   • _____ .

The value that occurs most often in a data set is called the **mode**.

7. What is the mode of the presidents' ages at inauguration?

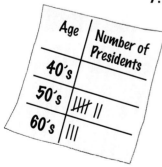

Jamaal thought it would be better to divide the ages into groups first and then look at what that might tell him. He made a table and tallied the ages of the first 10 presidents.

8. **a.** Copy Jamaal's table into your notebook and finish it. What does it tell you about the ages?

   b. Compare Jamaal's table to Sarah's graph.

Unfortunately, you cannot see the exact ages with Jamaal's method. One way to tally the ages so that you can see all of the numbers is to use a **stem-and-leaf plot**.

In a stem-and-leaf plot, each number is split into two parts, in this case a tens digit and a ones digit.

The first age in the list is 57. This would be written as:

$$5 \mid 7$$

You can make a stem-and-leaf plot like this one by going through the list of presidents on pages 51 and 52 and splitting each age into a tens digit and a ones digit.

Presidents' Ages at Inauguration
4 | 9 8 6 9 7 2
5 | 7 7 7 8 7 4 1 0 2 6 4 1 5 5 4 1 6 5 1 4 1
6 | 1 1 8 4 5
Key: 5 | 7 means 57 years

Note: So that everyone can read your diagram, you should always include a key like the one in the bottom corner, explaining what the numbers mean.

In the stem-and-leaf plot above, 4 | 9 8 6 9 7 2 stands for six presidents who were ages 49, 48, 46, 49, 47, and 42 at inauguration. All the ages at inauguration have been recorded except the last 11.

9. **a.** Copy and finish the stem-and-leaf plot. (You will start with Harry S. Truman.) Make sure you show the ages of all 43 presidents.

   b. Compare this stem-and-leaf plot to Jamaal's table on page 53. How are they different?

10. **Reflect** Why do you think this diagram is called a stem-and-leaf plot?

Harry S. Truman
(1884–1972)

Histograms

**Presidents' Ages
at Inauguration**

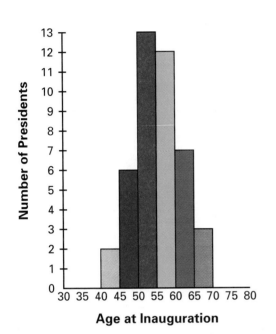

Number of Presidents

Age at Inauguration

This graph is called a **histogram**. It is a histogram of the ages of the presidents of the United States at inauguration.

In this histogram, the ages have been put into groups spanning five years, so the width of each bar is 5 years. Ages 50 through 54, for example, are in the same group.

11. a. Can you tell just by looking at the histogram how many presidents were 57 years old when they were inaugurated?

Activity

Your Teacher's Head

- Without measuring, estimate the length (in centimeters) of your teacher's head. Then collect the estimates from your classmates and make a histogram of the data. You will need to decide on a width for the bars.

- Now look at the collected data and decide whether to change your guess about the length of your teacher's head. When the class has agreed on a length, find out how close the real length is to the class guess.

Comparing Two Schools (page 1)

At Greenfield Middle School, $\frac{2}{3}$ of the students are female.
At Brendel Middle School, $\frac{5}{8}$ of the students are female.
To determine which school has a larger fraction of female
students you can think of two bars with the same
number of segments. Here you can use 24 segments.

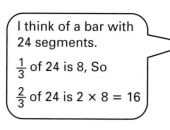

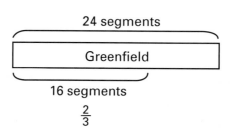

1. a. Complete the bar for Brendel Middle School.

b. Which school has the larger fraction of female
students?

c. Why are 24 segments handy? What other
number of segments would have worked too?

_____ segments

2. For each of the following categories, determine
which school has the larger fraction of students.

a. Students Transported by Bus

Greenfield, $\frac{5}{6}$ of the students

Brendel, $\frac{3}{4}$ of the students

b. Seventh-Grade Students

Greenfield, $\frac{1}{4}$ of the students

Brendel, $\frac{2}{5}$ of the students

Gina uses a ratio table to compare fractions. Here is her work for comparing $\frac{5}{6}$ and $\frac{3}{4}$.

$\frac{5}{6}$:

Part	5	10	
Whole	6	12	

$\frac{3}{4}$:

Part	3	6	9
Whole	4	8	12

3. Compare her ratio table strategy with the segmented bars you used to solve problem 2a on the previous page. What do you notice?

4. Compare the following pairs of fractions and circle the larger fraction. You may choose any strategy you like. Show your work or reasoning.

   a. $\frac{1}{4}$ and $\frac{1}{5}$

   b. $\frac{2}{3}$ and $\frac{5}{8}$

   c. $\frac{2}{3}$ and $\frac{4}{9}$

   d. $\frac{1}{3}$ and $\frac{2}{5}$

   e. $\frac{2}{3}$ and $\frac{1}{2}$

   f. $\frac{3}{8}$ and $\frac{1}{4}$

   g. $\frac{3}{4}$ and $\frac{4}{5}$

   h. $\frac{3}{5}$ and $\frac{3}{4}$

   i. $\frac{4}{9}$ and $\frac{1}{3}$

What Difference?

Among Ms. Washington's students, $\frac{2}{3}$ of the class participate in a sport. Of those students, one-fourth of them play basketball. What fraction of Ms. Washington's class participates in a sport other than basketball? Here is how Thomas solved this problem.

I think of a class with 24 students. Then $\frac{2}{3}$ of 24 is 16, so 16 students play sports.

And $\frac{1}{4}$ of 16 is 4, so 4 play basketball.

That means that 12 play another sport, and 12 out of 24 is the same as $\frac{1}{2}$, so the answer is $\frac{1}{2}$.

24 students   **12 play sports**

4 play basketball

1. Among Mr. Guiford's students, $\frac{3}{4}$ of the class participate in a sport. If $\frac{1}{3}$ of those students play basketball, what fraction of the class participates in a sport other than basketball?

2. At Jefferson Middle School, $\frac{1}{3}$ of the students study a foreign language. If $\frac{2}{9}$ of the students study Japanese, what fraction of the students study a foreign language other than Japanese?

3. Solve the following subtraction problems.

   a. $\frac{3}{8} - \frac{1}{4} =$ **f.** $\frac{6}{8} - \frac{2}{3} =$

   b. $\frac{5}{8} - \frac{2}{4} =$ **g.** $\frac{2}{3} - \frac{1}{2} =$

   c. $\frac{1}{4} - \frac{1}{6} =$ **h.** $\frac{4}{8} - \frac{3}{9} =$

   d. $\frac{4}{5} - \frac{2}{3} =$ **i.** $\frac{4}{9} - \frac{2}{6} =$

   e. $\frac{2}{3} - \frac{2}{5} =$

Key to Success

BRITANNICA
Mathematics
in
Context

Level 3

Lesson
Six
Activities

Histograms and the Mean

Hand Spans

For pianists, having large hand spans can make playing some pieces of music much easier. Hand span is the distance from the tip of the thumb to the tip of the little finger when the hand is extended.

Here are the hand spans of eleven pianists (in centimeters).

17, 21, 22, 19, 24, 19, 17, 19, 20, 21, 20

1. **a.** In what interval do the majority of these hand spans fit?

   b. How does your hand span compare to the ones of the eleven pianists?

   c. Draw a hand span to scale that you think is typical for a pianist.

Sergei Rachmaninoff (1873–1943), a Russian composer, had a very large hand span. He had a span of 12 white notes and could play a left-hand chord of C, E flat, G, C, and G.

Activity

Use a long string to measure the hand spans of four or five students. Then use the string to estimate the average hand span. Be ready to explain to the class how you made your estimation.

22 cm

24 cm

17 cm

20 cm

17 cm

Fathers and Sons Revisited

Recall Tiwanda's statement from page 3:
"I can say that the sons were generally taller than their fathers, because the total height of all of the fathers is 72,033 inches. The total height of all of the sons is 73,126 inches."

2. **a.** If you divide the fathers' total height equally over all 1,064 fathers, what would you estimate for the height of a father?

   This number is called the *mean height* of the fathers. The **mean** is one measure of the center of a list of numbers.

   b. Calculate the mean height of the sons.

   c. The mean height of the sons is larger than the mean height of the fathers. Is this information enough to conclude that sons are generally taller than their fathers?

   d. What other number(s) might you also give, with the mean, to help convince someone that the sons were generally taller than their fathers?

Mai-Li calculated the mean height of the fathers correctly, but when she looked at the data set, she was surprised to see that only 18 fathers were exactly the mean height.

3. **a.** **Reflect** Are you also surprised by this fact? Explain why or why not.

   b. Does the mean seem to be a typical height in each case? Why or why not?

Water

Students at Fontana Middle School surveyed their classmates to find out approximately how many bottles of water students drink per day.

4. **a.** Approximately how many 12-ounce bottles of water do you drink per day?

   b. Do you think this number is typical? Explain.

In a sixth-grade class, the students at Fontana Middle School found the following results.

> **Number of Bottles of Water Sixth Graders Drink Per Day**
>
> 0, 1, 5, 1, 0, 0, 5, 4, 5, 0, 4, 2, 1, 3, 3, 0, 1, 0, 4, 5, 5, 2, 4, 5

5. **a.** Find the mean number of bottles of water the students in this class drink per day. Show how you calculated the mean.

   b. Do you think that the mean is a good way to describe the amount of water a sixth grader drinks per day? Why or why not?

Here are the results of the survey for an eighth-grade class.

Number of Bottles of Water Eighth Graders Drink Per Day

1, 0, 0, 0, 1, 2, 3, 4, 2, 0, 1, 1, 0, 0, 13, 3, 2, 2, 0, 0, 1, 11, 1, 2, 3, 3, 13

6. a. To get a picture of the data, make a histogram of the number of bottles of water the eighth graders drink per day. (Use **Student Activity Sheet 1.**)

   b. How does water consumption for the eighth-grade class compare to that for the sixth-grade class?

   c. Estimate the mean from the eighth-grade histogram and then calculate the mean from the data. How well did you estimate?

   d. Would it be useful to compare the data for the two classes, using the mean? Why or why not?

Sometimes the mean is given together with the range. The **range** is the difference between the highest data point and the lowest data point.

   e. Using the means and the ranges, write a few sentences comparing the number of bottles of water the sixth- and eighth-grade classes drink each day.

Sun and Snow

Weather reports often give the average temperature for a city or region of the country. The mean yearly temperature in San Francisco, California, is 58° Fahrenheit (F), and the mean in Louisville, Kentucky, is 57°F.

7. Reflect Do you think using the mean yearly temperatures is a good way to compare the typical temperatures for the two cities? Why or why not?

Louisville, Kentucky

In the table, you see the mean monthly temperatures for Louisville in degrees Fahrenheit.

Month	Jan	Feb	Mar	Apr	May	Jun	Jul	Aug	Sept	Oct	Nov	Dec
°F	33	38	47	56	66	74	78	77	70	59	48	38

The mean monthly temperatures in San Francisco range from 52°F to 64°F.

8. Make a table like the one shown above and write down what the mean monthly temperatures in San Francisco might be.

9. a. Based on all the information given, how do you think the temperatures in the two cities compare?

  b. **Reflect** Explain why it is important to know the range in addition to the mean.

BRITANNICA
Mathematics
in
Context

Key to Success

In order to solve the problems on this page, you may use the ratio table given with each problem. If necessary, add extra columns.

1. A fruit stand sells three apples for $2. How much would you have to pay for 12 apples?

Apples	3			
Dollars	2.00			

2. What would you have to pay for 33 apples? Choose your own method to calculate the answer.

Apples	3				
Dollars	2.00				

3. The fruit stand sells five California oranges for $3.75. How much would you have to pay for 35 oranges?

Oranges	5			
Dollars	3.75			

4. Four Florida oranges sell for $2.50. You have $10 to spend. How many oranges can you buy?

Oranges	4			
Dollars	2.50			

5. Two cantaloupes sell for $3. How many cantaloupes can you buy for $7.50?

Cantaloupes	2			
Dollars	3.00			

How Do You Do It?

Using ratio tables is a convenient way to solve some problems. You may have discovered that the ratio table offers a handy way to write down the intermediate steps you take to solve a problem.

There are several ways to use existing numbers to find new numbers. Here are some examples of operations you can use.

1. Fill in the missing numbers.

a. Doubling or Multiplying by Two

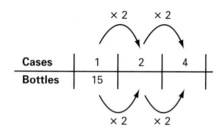

b. Halving or Dividing By Two

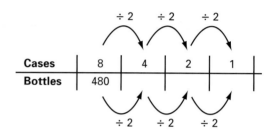

c. Times Ten

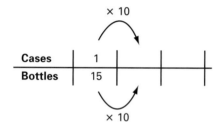

d. Multiplying

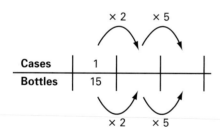

e. Dividing

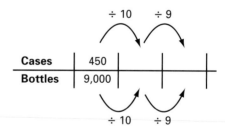

f. Adding Columns

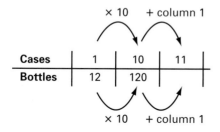

g. Subtracting Columns

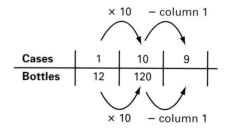

Key to Success

BRITANNICA
Mathematics
in
Context

Level 3

Lesson
Seven
Activities

Box Plots and the Median

The United States

A path from the parking area to Mount Rushmore National Monument in South Dakota displays the growth of the United States. The flags of all of the 50 states are along the path. A sign for each state shows the year that the state entered the Union.

This table shows the year of admission to the Union for each state.

1.	Delaware	1787	26.	Michigan	1837
2.	Pennsylvania	1787	27.	Florida	1845
3.	New Jersey	1787	28.	Texas	1845
4.	Georgia	1788	29.	Iowa	1846
5.	Connecticut	1788	30.	Wisconsin	1848
6.	Massachusetts	1788	31.	California	1850
7.	Maryland	1788	32.	Minnesota	1858
8.	South Carolina	1788	33.	Oregon	1859
9.	New Hampshire	1788	34.	Kansas	1861
10.	Virginia	1788	35.	West Virginia	1863
11.	New York	1788	36.	Nevada	1864
12.	North Carolina	1789	37.	Nebraska	1867
13.	Rhode Island	1790	38.	Colorado	1876
14.	Vermont	1791	39.	North Dakota	1889
15.	Kentucky	1792	40.	South Dakota	1889
16.	Tennessee	1796	41.	Montana	1889
17.	Ohio	1803	42.	Washington	1889
18.	Louisiana	1812	43.	Idaho	1890
19.	Indiana	1816	44.	Wyoming	1890
20.	Mississippi	1817	45.	Utah	1896
21.	Illinois	1818	46.	Oklahoma	1907
22.	Alabama	1819	47.	New Mexico	1912
23.	Maine	1820	48.	Arizona	1912
24.	Missouri	1821	49.	Alaska	1959
25.	Arkansas	1836	50.	Hawaii	1959

In 1787, Delaware became the first state. By 1959, there were 50 states in the United States. So the nation took 172 years to add all 50 states.

Jill says, "It looks like the growth of the United States was not steady. There were times when it grew quickly and times when it grew slowly."

1. Can you be more specific than Jill? Look at the list of states and write a few sentences in your own words to describe how the United States grew.

A weekly magazine has organized a contest with the title "Write about the Growth of the United States." The rules state, "Often pictures tell more than words. You may use a picture or diagram to help people understand what you are saying."

Anita made the following dot plot of the data. (You can see the enlarged plot on **Student Activity Sheet 1**.)

Number of States Entering the Union

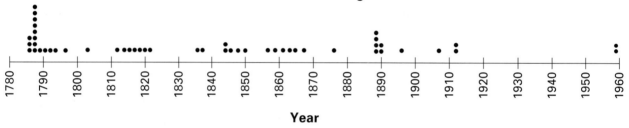

Year

2. **a.** By what year had half of the 50 states entered the United States?

   b. Draw a line to show your answer to part **a** on the dot plot on **Student Activity Sheet 1**.

The year that splits the group of 50 states into two groups of equal size is called the **median.**

Anita says, "I could use either 1836 or 1837 as the median of the group."

3. **a.** What does Anita mean?

   b. How would you choose a year for the median?

The median value is the value in the middle of a set of ordered numbers. If there is an even number of values, the median is the mean of the two middle values.

4. **a.** What year is halfway between 1787 and 1959? How does this year compare to the median year for the states?

   b. What does the median year tell you about the growth of the United States?

Note that the middle of the range is not the same as the median.

   c. **Reflect** Explain the difference between the middle of the range and the median.

To look more closely at how the United States grew, you can separate the states into four groups, each with an equal number of states. These groups are shown on the dot plot.

Number of States Entering the Union

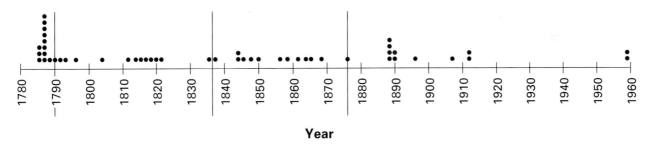

Year

5. **a.** Use **Student Activity Sheet 1** to verify that the states have been divided into four equal groups.

   b. What years divide the data into the four groups? Write them on the plot. Did a state enter the Union during any of those years?

   c. Once again, write a few lines about the growth of the United States. This time, use the dates you wrote on the plot to answer part **b**.

Lesson Seven Activities

Back to Pearson and Lee

Here are a histogram and a **box plot** of the heights of fathers in the Pearson and Lee study. The data to create these graphs were obtained from **Appendix B**.

6. **a.** Explain why the whiskers of the box plot are relatively long compared to the length of the box.

   b. Reflect Do you like the box plot or the histogram better? Why?

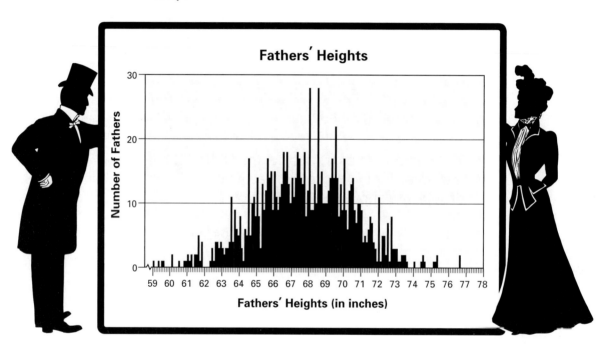

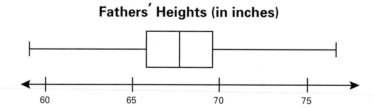

To compare the heights of fathers and sons, box plots can be used.

A box plot clearly shows the spread in heights. Placing the two plots one above the other makes comparing the heights of fathers and sons easy.

The data to create the sons'
box plot were obtained from
Appendix C.

Here are the two box plots.

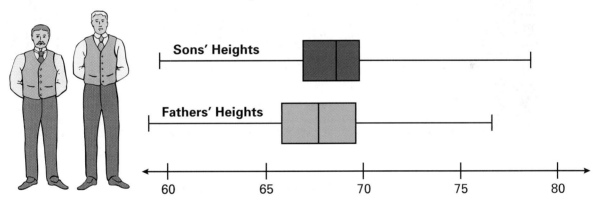

7. a. How do the box plots support the statement that sons are
generally taller than their fathers?

b. What can you tell about the tallest 25% of the sons compared
to the tallest 25% of the fathers?

c. Write some other statements based on the box plots.

Fathers Sorted by Height (in inches)

59.0	63.5	64.5	65.1	65.7	66.2	66.7	67.2	67.6	68.0	68.5	68.8	69.3	69.8	70.4	71.0	72.2
59.3	63.5	64.5	65.1	65.7	66.2	66.7	67.2	67.6	68.0	68.5	68.9	69.4	69.8	70.4	71.0	72.2
59.5	63.5	64.5	65.1	65.7	66.2	66.7	67.2	67.6	68.0	68.5	68.9	69.4	69.8	70.4	71.0	72.2
59.6	63.5	64.5	65.1	65.7	66.2	66.7	67.2	67.6	68.0	68.5	68.9	69.4	69.8	70.4	71.0	72.2
60.1	63.5	64.5	65.1	65.7	66.2	66.7	67.2	67.6	68.0	68.5	68.9	69.4	69.8	70.4	71.0	72.3
60.1	63.5	64.5	65.2	65.7	66.2	66.7	67.2	67.6	68.0	68.5	68.9	69.4	69.8	70.4	[950]71.0	72.3
60.5	63.5	64.5	65.2	65.7	66.3	66.7	67.2	67.6	68.0	68.5	[700]68.9	69.4	69.8	70.4	71.0	72.3
60.8	63.5	64.5	65.2	65.7	66.3	66.7	67.2	67.6	68.0	68.5	68.9	69.4	69.8	70.4	71.0	72.3
60.9	63.5	64.5	65.3	65.7	66.3	66.7	[450]67.2	67.6	68.0	68.5	68.9	69.4	69.8	70.4	71.1	72.3
61.0	63.5	64.5	65.3	65.7	66.3	66.7	67.2	67.6	68.0	68.5	68.9	69.4	69.9	70.4	71.1	72.4
61.0	63.5	64.5	[200]65.3	65.8	66.3	66.7	67.2	67.6	68.0	68.5	68.9	69.4	69.9	70.4	71.1	72.4
61.1	63.6	64.5	65.3	65.8	66.3	66.7	67.2	67.6	68.0	68.5	69.0	69.4	69.9	70.4	71.1	72.5
61.2	63.6	64.6	65.3	65.8	66.3	66.7	67.2	67.7	68.0	68.5	69.0	69.4	69.9	70.5	71.2	72.5
61.2	63.6	64.6	65.3	65.8	66.3	66.8	67.3	67.7	68.0	68.5	69.0	69.4	69.9	70.5	71.2	72.5
61.4	63.6	64.6	65.3	65.8	66.3	66.8	67.3	67.7	68.0	68.5	69.0	69.4	69.9	70.5	71.2	72.5
61.4	63.7	64.6	65.3	65.8	66.3	66.8	67.3	67.7	68.1	68.5	69.0	69.5	69.9	70.5	71.2	72.5
61.5	63.7	64.6	65.3	65.8	66.3	66.8	67.3	67.7	68.1	68.5	69.0	69.5	69.9	70.5	71.2	72.5
61.5	63.7	64.7	65.3	65.8	66.4	66.8	67.3	67.7	68.1	68.5	69.0	69.5	69.9	70.5	71.3	72.5
61.6	63.7	64.7	65.3	65.8	66.4	66.8	67.3	67.7	68.1	68.5	69.0	69.5	70.0	[900]70.5	71.3	72.6
61.6	63.7	64.7	65.3	65.8	66.4	66.8	67.3	67.7	68.1	[650]68.5	69.0	69.5	70.0	70.5	71.3	72.7
61.6	63.7	64.7	65.3	65.8	66.4	66.8	67.3	67.7	68.1	68.5	69.0	69.5	70.0	70.5	71.3	72.7
61.6	63.7	64.7	65.4	65.8	66.4	[400]66.8	67.3	67.7	68.1	68.5	69.1	69.5	70.0	70.5	71.4	72.7
61.6	63.7	64.7	65.4	65.8	66.4	66.8	67.3	67.7	68.1	68.5	69.1	69.5	70.0	70.5	71.4	72.7
61.7	63.7	[150]64.7	65.4	65.8	66.4	66.8	67.3	67.7	68.1	68.5	69.1	69.5	70.0	70.5	71.4	72.7
61.8	63.8	64.7	65.4	65.8	66.4	66.8	67.3	67.7	68.2	68.5	69.1	69.5	70.0	70.5	71.4	72.7
61.8	63.8	64.7	65.4	65.9	66.4	66.8	67.3	67.7	68.2	68.5	69.1	69.5	70.0	70.5	71.4	72.7
61.8	63.8	64.7	65.4	65.9	66.4	66.9	67.3	67.7	68.2	68.6	69.1	69.5	70.0	70.6	71.4	72.7
61.8	63.8	64.8	65.4	65.9	66.4	66.9	67.3	67.7	68.2	68.6	69.1	69.5	70.0	70.6	71.5	72.8
62.3	63.8	64.8	65.4	65.9	66.4	66.9	67.3	67.7	68.2	68.6	69.1	69.5	70.0	70.6	71.5	72.8
62.4	63.8	64.8	65.4	65.9	66.4	66.9	67.3	67.7	68.2	68.6	69.1	69.5	70.0	70.6	71.5	72.8
62.4	63.9	64.8	65.5	65.9	66.5	66.9	67.3	67.8	68.2	68.6	69.1	69.5	[850]70.0	70.6	71.5	72.9
62.4	63.9	64.8	65.5	65.9	66.5	66.9	67.4	67.8	68.2	68.6	69.1	69.5	70.0	70.6	71.5	72.9
62.5	63.9	64.8	65.5	65.9	66.5	66.9	67.4	67.8	[600]68.2	68.6	69.1	69.5	70.0	70.6	71.5	73.0
62.6	63.9	64.8	65.5	65.9	66.5	66.9	67.4	67.8	68.3	68.6	69.2	69.5	70.0	70.6	71.5	73.0
62.6	63.9	64.8	65.5	66.0	66.5	66.9	67.4	67.8	68.3	68.6	69.2	69.5	70.0	70.6	71.5	73.0
62.6	64.0	64.8	65.5	66.0	[350]66.5	66.9	67.4	67.8	68.3	68.6	69.2	69.6	70.1	70.7	71.6	73.0
62.6	[100]64.0	64.8	65.5	66.0	66.5	66.9	67.4	67.8	68.3	68.6	69.2	69.5	70.1	70.7	71.6	73.1
62.7	64.0	64.8	65.5	66.0	66.5	67.0	67.4	67.8	68.3	68.6	69.2	69.6	70.1	70.7	71.6	73.2
62.7	64.0	64.9	65.5	66.0	66.5	67.0	67.4	67.9	68.3	68.6	69.2	69.6	70.1	70.7	71.6	73.3
62.7	64.0	64.9	65.5	66.0	66.5	67.0	67.4	67.9	68.3	68.7	69.2	69.6	70.1	70.7	71.6	73.3
62.7	64.0	64.9	65.5	66.0	66.5	67.0	67.4	67.9	68.3	68.7	69.2	69.6	70.1	70.7	71.6	73.4
62.8	64.0	64.9	65.5	66.0	66.5	67.0	67.4	67.9	68.3	68.7	69.2	69.6	70.1	70.7	71.6	73.4
62.8	64.0	64.9	65.6	66.0	66.5	67.0	67.4	67.9	68.3	68.7	69.2	69.6	70.1	70.8	71.7	[1,050]73.5
62.8	64.1	64.9	65.6	66.0	66.5	67.0	67.4	67.9	68.3	68.7	69.2	[800]69.6	70.1	70.8	71.7	73.5
62.9	64.1	64.9	65.6	66.0	66.5	67.0	67.4	67.9	68.3	68.7	69.2	69.6	70.2	70.8	71.7	73.6
62.9	64.1	64.9	65.6	66.0	66.5	67.0	67.4	[550]67.9	68.3	68.7	69.2	69.6	70.2	70.8	71.7	74.0
62.9	64.2	65.0	65.6	66.0	66.5	67.0	67.4	67.9	68.4	68.7	69.2	69.6	70.2	70.8	71.8	74.4
62.9	64.3	65.0	65.6	[300]66.0	66.6	67.0	67.4	67.9	68.4	68.7	69.3	69.6	70.2	70.8	71.8	74.5
63.0	64.3	65.0	65.6	66.0	66.6	67.0	67.5	67.9	68.4	68.7	69.3	69.6	70.2	70.8	71.8	74.5
[50]63.0	64.3	65.0	65.6	66.1	66.6	67.0	67.5	67.9	68.4	68.7	69.3	69.6	70.2	70.8	71.9	74.6
63.0	64.3	65.0	65.6	66.1	66.6	67.0	67.5	68.0	68.4	68.7	69.3	69.6	70.3	70.8	72.0	75.1
63.1	64.3	65.0	65.6	66.1	66.6	67.1	67.5	68.0	68.4	68.7	69.3	69.7	70.3	70.8	72.0	75.2
63.1	64.3	65.0	65.6	66.1	66.6	67.1	67.5	68.0	68.4	68.7	69.3	69.7	70.3	70.9	72.0	75.3
63.2	64.4	65.0	65.6	66.1	66.6	67.1	67.5	68.0	68.4	68.7	69.3	69.7	70.3	70.9	72.0	75.3
63.2	64.4	65.0	65.6	66.1	66.6	67.1	67.5	68.0	68.4	68.8	69.3	69.7	70.3	70.9	[1,000]72.0	76.6
63.2	64.4	65.0	65.6	66.1	66.6	67.1	67.5	68.0	68.4	68.8	69.3	69.7	70.3	70.9	72.0	76.6
63.3	64.4	65.0	65.6	66.1	66.6	67.1	67.5	68.0	68.4	68.8	69.3	69.7	70.3	70.9	72.0	
63.3	64.4	65.0	65.6	66.1	66.6	67.1	67.5	68.0	68.4	68.8	[750]69.3	69.7	70.3	70.9	72.0	
63.3	64.5	65.0	65.6	66.1	66.7	67.1	67.5	68.0	68.4	68.8	69.3	69.7	70.3	70.9	72.0	
63.4	64.5	65.0	65.7	66.1	66.7	67.1	67.5	68.0	68.4	68.8	69.3	69.8	70.3	70.9	72.0	
63.4	64.5	65.1	65.7	66.2	66.7	67.1	67.5	68.0	68.4	68.8	69.3	69.8	70.3	70.9	72.1	
63.4	64.5	65.1	65.7	66.2	66.7	67.2	67.6	68.0	68.5	68.8	69.3	69.8	70.4	71.0	72.2	

Appendix C Pearson and Lee's Data

Sons Sorted by Height (in inches)

59.7	64.5	65.5	66.3	66.8	67.3	67.7	68.0	68.4	68.8	69.3	69.7	70.2	70.8	71.3	72.0	73.4
59.9	64.5	65.5	66.3	66.8	67.3	67.7	68.0	68.4	68.9	69.3	69.7	70.2	70.8	71.3	72.0	73.5
60.9	64.5	65.5	66.3	66.8	67.3	67.7	68.0	68.4	68.9	69.3	69.7	70.2	70.8	71.3	72.1	73.5
61.4	64.5	65.5	66.3	66.9	67.3	67.7	68.0	68.4	68.9	69.3	69.7	70.2	70.8	71.3	72.1	73.5
62.0	64.6	65.5	66.4	66.9	67.3	67.7	68.0	68.4	68.9	69.3	69.8	70.2	70.8	71.3	72.1 (950)	73.5
62.3	64.6	65.5	66.4	66.9	67.3	67.7	68.0	68.4	68.9	69.3	69.8	70.3	70.8	71.3	72.1	73.5
62.4	64.6	65.5	66.4	66.9	67.3	67.7	68.0	68.4	68.9	69.3	69.8 (700)	70.3	70.8	71.3	72.2	73.6
62.5	64.6	65.6	66.4	66.9	67.3	67.7	68.0	68.4	68.9	69.3	69.8	70.3	70.8	71.4	72.2	73.6
62.5	64.6	65.6	66.4	66.9	67.3	67.7	68.1 (450)	68.4	68.9	69.3	69.8	70.3	70.8	71.4	72.2	73.6
62.5	64.6	65.6	66.4	66.9	67.3	67.7	68.1	68.5	68.9	69.3	69.8	70.3	70.8	71.4	72.2	73.6
62.7	64.7	65.6	66.4 (200)	66.9	67.3	67.7	68.1	68.5	69.0	69.3	69.8	70.3	70.8	71.4	72.2	73.6
62.8	64.7	65.6	66.4	66.9	67.3	67.7	68.1	68.5	69.0	69.3	69.8	70.3	70.8	71.4	72.2	73.6
62.8	64.7	65.6	66.5	66.9	67.4	67.7	68.1	68.5	69.0	69.4	69.8	70.3	70.8	71.4	72.2	73.6
62.9	64.7	65.6	66.5	66.9	67.4	67.7	68.1	68.5	69.0	69.4	69.8	70.3	70.9	71.4	72.3	73.6
62.9	64.7	65.6	66.5	66.9	67.4	67.7	68.1	68.5	69.0	69.4	69.8	70.3	70.9	71.4	72.3	73.8
63.0	64.8	65.7	66.5	66.9	67.4	67.7	68.1	68.5	69.0	69.4	69.8	70.3	70.9	71.4	72.3	73.9
63.1	64.8	65.7	66.5	66.9	67.4	67.7	68.1	68.5	69.0	69.4	69.8	70.4	70.9	71.4	72.3	73.9
63.1	64.8	65.7	66.5	67.0	67.4	67.7	68.1	68.5	69.0	69.4	69.8	70.4	70.9	71.4 (900)	72.3	74.0
63.1	64.8	65.7	66.5	67.0	67.4	67.7	68.1	68.5	69.0	69.4	69.9	70.4	70.9	71.4	72.3	74.0
63.2	64.8	65.7	66.5	67.0	67.4	67.7	68.1	68.5	69.0	69.4 (650)	69.9	70.4	70.9	71.5	72.3	74.0
63.4	64.8	65.7	66.5	67.0	67.4	67.7	68.1	68.5	69.0	69.4	69.9	70.4	70.9	71.5	72.4	74.0
63.4	64.9	65.7	66.5	67.0	67.4	67.8 (400)	68.1	68.5	69.0	69.4	69.9	70.4	70.9	71.5	72.4	74.0
63.4	64.9	65.7	66.5	67.0	67.4	67.8	68.2	68.5	69.0	69.4	69.9	70.4	70.9	71.5	72.4	74.0
63.4	64.9	65.8 (150)	66.5	67.0	67.4	67.8	68.2	68.5	69.0	69.4	69.9	70.4	70.9	71.5	72.4	74.0
63.4	64.9	65.8	66.5	67.0	67.5	67.8	68.2	68.5	69.0	69.4	69.9	70.4	70.9	71.5	72.4	74.2
63.5	64.9	65.8	66.5	67.0	67.5	67.8	68.2	68.5	69.0	69.4	69.9	70.4	70.9	71.5	72.5	74.2
63.5	64.9	65.8	66.5	67.0	67.5	67.8	68.2	68.5	69.1	69.4	69.9	70.4	71.0	71.5	72.5	74.2
63.5	64.9	65.8	66.6	67.0	67.5	67.8	68.2	68.6	69.1	69.4	69.9	70.4	71.0	71.5	72.5	74.2
63.5	64.9	65.8	66.6	67.0	67.5	67.8	68.2	68.6	69.1	69.4	69.9	70.4	71.0	71.6	72.5	74.3
63.5	64.9	65.8	66.6	67.0	67.5	67.8	68.2	68.6	69.1	69.4	69.9	70.4	71.0	71.6	72.6	74.3
63.6	64.9	65.8	66.6	67.0	67.5	67.8	68.2	68.6	69.1	69.5	70.0	70.4	71.0 (850)	71.6	72.6	74.3
63.6	65.0	65.8	66.6	67.0	67.5	67.8	68.2	68.6	69.1	69.5	70.0	70.4	71.0	71.6	72.6	74.3
63.7	65.0	65.9	66.6	67.0	67.5	67.8	68.2	68.6	69.1 (600)	69.5	70.0	70.4	71.0	71.6	72.7	74.3
63.8	65.0	65.9	66.6	67.0	67.5	67.8	68.2	68.6	69.1	69.5	70.0	70.5	71.0	71.7	72.7	74.4
63.8	65.0	65.9	66.6	67.0	67.5 (350)	67.9	68.2	68.6	69.2	69.5	70.0	70.5	71.0	71.7	72.7	74.5
63.8	65.0	65.9	66.6	67.0	67.5	67.9	68.2	68.6	69.2	69.5	70.0	70.5	71.0	71.7	72.7	74.5
63.9	65.0 (100)	65.9	66.6	67.0	67.5	67.9	68.2	68.6	69.2	69.5	70.0	70.5	71.0	71.7	72.7	74.7
63.9	65.0	65.9	66.6	67.1	67.5	67.9	68.2	68.6	69.2	69.5	70.0	70.5	71.0	71.7	72.7	74.8
63.9	65.0	66.0	66.6	67.1	67.5	67.9	68.2	68.6	69.2	69.5	70.0	70.5	71.0	71.7	72.8	74.9
63.9	65.0	66.0	66.6	67.1	67.5	67.9	68.2	68.6	69.2	69.5	70.0	70.5	71.1	71.7	72.8	75.1
63.9	65.0	66.0	66.6	67.1	67.5	67.9	68.3	68.6	69.2	69.5	70.0	70.5	71.1	71.7	72.8	75.2
63.9	65.1	66.0	66.6	67.1	67.5	67.9	68.3	68.7	69.2	69.5	70.0	70.5	71.1	71.7	72.8	75.2 (1,050)
64.0	65.1	66.0	66.6	67.1	67.5	67.9	68.3	68.7	69.2	69.5	70.0	70.5	71.1	71.8	72.8	75.4
64.0	65.1	66.0	66.7	67.1	67.5	68.0	68.3	68.7	69.2	69.5	70.0	70.5 (800)	71.1	71.8	72.9	75.5
64.0	65.1	66.0	66.7	67.1	67.6	68.0	68.3	68.7	69.2	69.5	70.0	70.5	71.1	71.8	73.0	75.5
64.1	65.1	66.0	66.7	67.1	67.6	68.0	68.3	68.7 (550)	69.2	69.6	70.0	70.5	71.1	71.8	73.0	75.7
64.2	65.2	66.1	66.7	67.1	67.6	68.0	68.3	68.7	69.2	69.6	70.0	70.5	71.1	71.8	73.0	76.4
64.2	65.2	66.1	66.7	67.1 (300)	67.6	68.0	68.3	68.7	69.2	69.6	70.0	70.5	71.1	71.8	73.1	76.5
64.2	65.2	66.1	66.7	67.1	67.6	68.0	68.3	68.7	69.2	69.6	70.0	70.6	71.2	71.8	73.1	76.5
64.3 (50)	65.3	66.1	66.7	67.1	67.6	68.0	68.3	68.7	69.2	69.6	70.0	70.6	71.2	71.8	73.1	76.6
64.3	65.3	66.1	66.7	67.2	67.6	68.0	68.3	68.7	69.2	69.6	70.1	70.6	71.2	71.8	73.2	77.4
64.3	65.3	66.2	66.7	67.2	67.6	68.0	68.3	68.7	69.2	69.6	70.1	70.6	71.2	71.8	73.2	77.4
64.3	65.3	66.2	66.7	67.2	67.6	68.0	68.3	68.8	69.2	69.6	70.1	70.6	71.2	71.8	73.2	77.5
64.3	65.3	66.2	66.7	67.2	67.6	68.0	68.3	68.8	69.2	69.7	70.1	70.6	71.2	71.9	73.3	78.0
64.4	65.3	66.3	66.7	67.2	67.6	68.0	68.3	68.8	69.3	69.7	70.1	70.6	71.2	71.9	73.3 (1,000)	78.1
64.4	65.3	66.3	66.7	67.2	67.7	68.0	68.3	68.8	69.3	69.7	70.1	70.6	71.3	71.9	73.3	78.6
64.4	65.4	66.3	66.7	67.2	67.7	68.0	68.3	68.8	69.3	69.7	70.1 (750)	70.6	71.3	72.0	73.3	
64.4	65.4	66.3	66.8	67.2	67.7	68.0	68.4	68.8	69.3	69.7	70.1	70.7	71.3	72.0	73.3	
64.4	65.4	66.3	66.8	67.2	67.7	68.0	68.4 (500)	68.8	69.3	69.7	70.2	70.7	71.3	72.0	73.4	
64.4	65.4	66.3	66.8	67.2	67.7	68.0	68.4	68.8	69.3	69.7	70.2	70.7	71.3	72.0	73.4	
64.4	65.4	66.3	66.8 (250)	67.3	67.7	68.0	68.4	68.8	69.3	69.7	70.2	70.7	71.3	72.0	73.4	
64.4	65.4	66.3	66.8	67.3	67.7	68.0	68.4	68.8	69.3	69.7	70.2	70.7	71.3	72.0	73.4	
64.5	65.5	66.3	66.8	67.3	67.7	68.0	68.4	68.8	69.3	69.7	70.2	70.7	71.3	72.0	73.4	

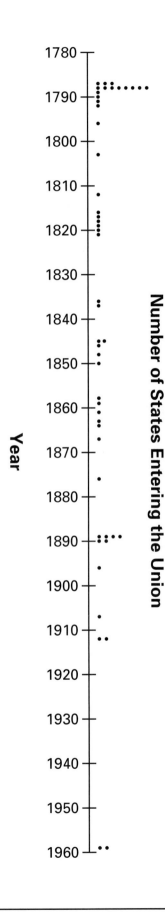

Key to Success

Multiplication and Division

Mr. Starks has an aquarium in his classroom. In order to find its volume, Mr. Starks's students first determine the aquarium's dimensions, as shown. Maya, Luisa, and Thomas each propose a different arrow string to find the aquarium's volume.

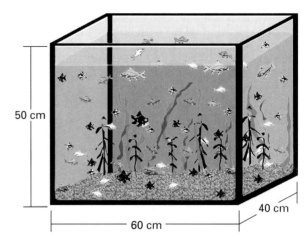

$60 \xrightarrow{\times 40} 2,400 \xrightarrow{\times 50} 120,000 \text{ cm}^3$

$60 \xrightarrow{\times 50} 3,000 \xrightarrow{\times 40} 120,000 \text{ cm}^3$

$60 \xrightarrow{\times 2,000} 120,000 \text{ cm}^3$

1. Compare the three arrow strings. How are the strategies the same? How are they different?

2. For each of the following arrow strings fill in the missing numbers. Then write another arrow string that shows an alternative way to calculate the answer.

   a. $8 \xrightarrow{\times 5} \underline{\quad} \xrightarrow{\times 4} \underline{\quad}$

   b. $32 \xrightarrow{\times 2} \underline{\quad} \xrightarrow{\times 5} \underline{\quad}$

   c. $50 \xrightarrow{\times 5} \underline{\quad} \xrightarrow{\div 4} \underline{\quad}$

   d. $750 \xrightarrow{\div 3} \underline{\quad} \xrightarrow{\times 2} \underline{\quad}$

   e. $1,050 \xrightarrow{\div 5} \underline{\quad} \xrightarrow{\div 2} \underline{\quad}$

   f. $9 \xrightarrow{\times 30} \underline{\quad} \xrightarrow{\div 30} \underline{\quad}$

   g. $123 \xrightarrow{\times 100} \underline{\quad} \xrightarrow{\times 5} \underline{\quad}$

3. Compare the following two arrow strings. Why are the final results different?

   $60 \xrightarrow{\times 5} \underline{\quad} \xrightarrow{+ 40} \underline{\quad}$ $60 \xrightarrow{+ 40} \underline{\quad} \xrightarrow{\times 5} \underline{\quad}$

Going Backwards

1. Find the result of each of the following arrow strings.

a. $38 \xrightarrow{+2} \_\_\_ \xrightarrow{\times 4} \_\_\_ \xrightarrow{-20} \_\_\_ \xrightarrow{\div 2} \_\_\_$

b. $70 \xrightarrow{+50} \_\_\_ \xrightarrow{-60} \_\_\_ \xrightarrow{\times 3} \_\_\_ \xrightarrow{-10} \_\_\_$

c. $5 \xrightarrow{\times 20} \_\_\_ \xrightarrow{-20} \_\_\_ \xrightarrow{\times 2} \_\_\_ \xrightarrow{\div 2} \_\_\_$

d. $606 \xrightarrow{+14} \_\_\_ \xrightarrow{\times 2} \_\_\_ \xrightarrow{-100} \_\_\_ \xrightarrow{+50} \_\_\_$

e. $1{,}000 \xrightarrow{\div 4} \_\_\_ \xrightarrow{\times 4} \_\_\_ \xrightarrow{-500} \_\_\_ \xrightarrow{+500} \_\_\_$

2. In each of the following arrow strings, the result is given. Fill in all of the missing numbers, especially the first number for each string.

a. $\_\_\_ \xrightarrow{\times 2} \_\_\_ \xrightarrow{\div 4} \_\_\_ \xrightarrow{-20} \_\_\_ \xrightarrow{\times 7} 35$

b. $\_\_\_ \xrightarrow{+19} \_\_\_ \xrightarrow{\times 2} \_\_\_ \xrightarrow{-100} \_\_\_ \xrightarrow{-95} 5$

c. $\_\_\_ \xrightarrow{+2} \_\_\_ \xrightarrow{\times 2} \_\_\_ \xrightarrow{-20} \_\_\_ \xrightarrow{\div 2} 40$

d. $\_\_\_ \xrightarrow{+50} \_\_\_ \xrightarrow{-10} \_\_\_ \xrightarrow{\div 3} \_\_\_ \xrightarrow{-2} 78$

e. $\_\_\_ \xrightarrow{+50} \_\_\_ \xrightarrow{\div 2} \_\_\_ \xrightarrow{-396} \_\_\_ \xrightarrow{\times 4} 16$

3. Make up your own arrow strings with the following results and number of arrows.

a. $\_\_\_ \longrightarrow \_\_\_ \longrightarrow \_\_\_ \longrightarrow \_\_\_ \longrightarrow 16$

b. $\_\_\_ \longrightarrow \_\_\_ \longrightarrow \_\_\_ \longrightarrow \_\_\_ \longrightarrow 20$

c. $\_\_\_ \longrightarrow \_\_\_ \longrightarrow \_\_\_ \longrightarrow \_\_\_ \longrightarrow 52$

4. Make up two arrow strings using other numbers, such as decimals or fraction or integers.

Key to Success

BRITANNICA
Mathematics
in
Context

Level 3

Lesson
Eight
Activities

Single Number Ratios

Car Pooling?

The students in Ms. Cole's science class are concerned about the air quality around Brooks Middle School. They noticed that smog frequently hangs over the area. They just finished a science project where they investigated the ways smog destroys plants, corrodes buildings and statues, and causes respiratory problems.

The students hypothesize that the city has so much smog because of the high number of cars on the roads. Students think there are so many cars because most people do not carpool. They want to find out if people carpool.

They set up an experiment to count the number of cars and people on the East Side Highway adjacent to the school.

One group spent exactly one minute and counted 10 cars and 12 people.

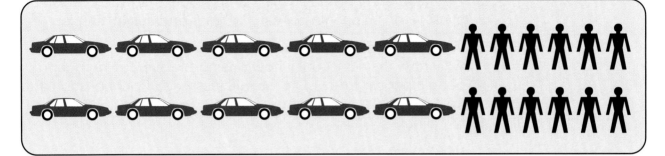

1. **a.** How many of these cars could have carried more than one person? Give all possible answers.

   b. Find the **average number** of people per car and explain how you found your answer.

At the same time, at a different point on the highway, a second group of students counts cars and people for two minutes. A third group counts cars and people for three minutes.

The second and third groups each calculate the average number of people per car. They are surprised to find that both groups got an average of 1.2 people per car.

2. How many cars and how many people might each group have counted?

Some students recommend that the average number of people per car should increase from 1.2 to 1.5 people per car.

   3. a. Find 5 different groups of cars and people that will give you an average of 1.5 people per car. Put your findings in a table.

   b. Work with a group of your classmates to make a poster that will show the city council how raising the average number of people per car from 1.2 to 1.5 will lessen traffic congestion and improve the quality of air.

Miles per Gallon

Another way to reduce air pollution is to encourage drivers to use automobiles that are more efficient. A local TV station decides to do a special series on how to reduce air pollution.

In one report, the newscaster mentions, "Cars with high gas mileage pollute less than cars with low gas mileage."

Gas mileage is the average number of miles (mi) a car can travel on 1 gallon (gal) of gasoline. It is represented by the **ratio** of miles per gallon (mpg).

John says, "My car's gas mileage is 25 mpg."

   4. How many miles can John travel on 12 gal of gas?

Cindy, Arturo, and Sheena see the report on TV. They decide to calculate their gas mileage to see whose car pollutes the least.

Cindy remembers that she drove 50 mi on 2.5 gal of gasoline. She creates the following **ratio table** on a scrap paper.

Miles	50	100	20	
Gallons	2.5	5	1	

Cindy says, "My gas mileage is 20 mpg."

5. Explain Cindy's calculation and answer.

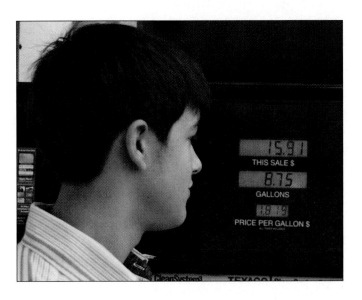

The last time Arturo filled up his car, he had driven 203 mi on 8.75 gal of gas.

6. Explain whether Arturo's gas mileage will be more or less than Cindy's gas mileage.

Arturo set up this ratio table to calculate his gas mileage.

Number of Miles	203	2,030	20,300	
Number of Gallons	8.75	87.5	875	

7. a. What did Arturo do in his ratio table to make the number of gallons a whole number?

b. Calculate Arturo 's gas mileage.

Sheena traveled 81.2 mi on 3.75 gal of gas.

8. Compare the gas mileage of Sheena's, Arturo 's and Cindy's cars. What conclusions can you draw?

Miles per Hour

It took Sheena 2 hours to travel 81.2 mi. Sheena used a ratio table to calculate the average number of miles she drove per hour. Here is Sheena's scrap of paper.

Miles	81.2	812	406	40.6
Hours	2	20	10	1

9. a. Explain Sheena's calculation method.

   b. What is the average number of miles Sheena drove per hour?

   c. How would *you* calculate the average number of miles per hour for Sheena?

The average number of miles per hour is called the **average speed**. Average speed is expressed in miles per hour (mi/h).

Average speed is expressed as a single number.

Mr. Martin's biology class is starting a school garden. They will be ordering plants by the box from a nursery. Mr. Martin asked the class to figure out how many tomato plants are in 16 boxes if one box contains 35 plants.

Three students—Darrell, Tasha, and Carla—solved the problem using ratio tables, but each student used a different table.

1. Darrell solved the problem as shown below.
   Explain Darrell's solution.

Boxes	1	2	3	4	5	6	7	8	16
Plants	35	70	105	140	175	210	245	280	560

2. Tasha solved the problem as shown below.
   Explain Tasha's solution.

Boxes	1	2	4	8	16
Plants	35	70	140	280	560

3. Carla solved the problem as shown below.
   Explain Carla's solution.

Boxes	1	10	2	6	16
Plants	35	350	70	210	560

Plants II (page 2)

4. Think of your own way to use a ratio table to figure out how many tomato plants are in 16 boxes with 35 tomato plants in each box. Show your solution in the table below. You may add as many columns as you need to the table.

Boxes	1				
Tomato Plants	35				

5. Cactus plants are shipped 45 pots to a box. If Mr. Martin's class orders 360 cactus plants, how many boxes will they get? Show your strategy using the following ratio table.

Boxes						
Cactuses						

6. Mr. Martin's students decide that they need 675 cactus plants. How many boxes will arrive?

Boxes						
Cactuses						

7. Rose bushes are shipped in boxes of 15. Mr. Martin's class orders 255 rose bushes. How many boxes is this?

Boxes					
Roses					

8. Strawberry plants are shipped in boxes of 70. If Mr. Martin's class orders 980 strawberry plants, how many boxes will arrive?

Boxes					
Strawberry Plants					

Key to Success

BRITANNICA
Mathematics
in
Context

Level 3

Lesson
Nine
Activities

Different Kinds of Ratios

Too Fast

The citizens of Wrigley are concerned about the number of people who speed through town. The local police have identified the four worst areas for speeding. The city council has agreed to install traffic lights to slow down the speeding cars.

At the present time, there is only enough money in the budget to install one traffic light. The council asks the police to decide which area needs the traffic light the most. The police make plans to study the situation and give a report at the next council meeting.

In order to monitor the number of drivers who speed through the four areas of town, the police set up a device to count and record the speed of passing cars.

Below is a chart showing the count at each area during a one-hour period in the morning.

	Speeders	Non-Speeders
Area 1	11	15
Area 2	42	20
Area 3	30	29
Area 4	4	0

1. a. Compare the results from these four areas of town.

   b. What recommendation would you make to the city council?

Suppose the police found another area of town where they suspect a lot of speeding takes place. When they count the cars and figure out how many people speed in this area, they find that the ratio of speeders to non-speeders is one to three, or 1:3.

2. Will this change the recommendation you made in problem 1b? Why or why not?

A neighboring town, Brighton, uses a sign on the highway. The sign constantly shows the **percent** of cars that pass the sign that are within the speed limit.

3. **a.** Why do you think the city put up this sign, and why do you think the sign shows the percent of drivers who are not speeding?

   b. How is percent related to ratio?

   c. Suppose the next car that passes the sign is speeding. How will the percent on the sign change? Explain your answer.

4. **a.** According to the sign, what part of the total number of cars was speeding?

   b. Suppose 269 cars have passed the sign shown. Estimate the number of cars that were speeding.

One local TV station covered the problem of speeding on the six o'clock news. The report gave some statistics to emphasize the seriousness of the situation.

> The police reported that on Highway 19, two cars were speeding for every three that were not speeding.

5. Can you conclude that over half of the cars were speeding on Highway 19? Why or why not?

Another TV station picked up the story. The newscaster from this station wanted to describe the speeding situation on Highway 19 in terms of percents.

6. What percents could be used?

The speed limit on Highway 19 where the sign is located is 55 mi/h. The sign is reset to zero at two o'clock every morning. The table below shows the speed of the first four cars that pass the sign after it was reset.

Car	Time	Speed (in mi/h)
1	2:00 AM	53
2	2:02 AM	60
3	2:03 AM	55
4	2:05 AM	52
5	2:10 AM	

7. a. What percent did the sign display after the first car passed the sign?

b. What percent did the sign display after the fourth car passed?

c. After the fifth car passes, the sign can display two possible percents. Explain why this is the case and calculate these percents.

Percent

One way to find a percent is to use the relationship between fractions and percents.

For example, if $\frac{1}{2}$ of the cars were speeding, 50% were speeding.

8. Write all of the relationships between fractions and percents that you know.

Joshua has to calculate the percentage of cars not speeding. 55 out of 76 cars were not speeding as they drove past the sign. Using his calculator, he got the decimal 0.7236842 as a result.

9. a. What did Joshua enter in his calculator to get this result?

   b. What does the number Joshua got as a result mean?

   c. Explain how Joshua can use the decimal to determine the percent of cars not speeding.

Part-Part and Part-Whole

Ms. Humphrey, 28 days

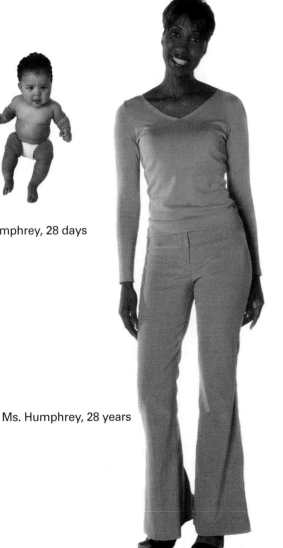

Ms. Humphrey, 28 years

These two photos show Ms. Humphrey as a baby and as an adult.

When Ms. Humphrey was a baby, her height was 60 cm and her head was 15 cm long.

10. a. As a baby, how long was her body (not including the head)?

   b. What was Ms. Humphrey's head-to-body ratio as a baby?

   c. What was her head-to-height ratio?

Now that she is an adult, Ms. Humphrey's height is 155 cm, and her head is 27 cm long.

11. a. As Ms. Humphrey grew up, what happened to the size of her head in relation to her height?

    b. Compare Ms. Humphrey's head-to-body and head-to-height ratio as a baby and as an adult. What do you notice? Describe your findings.

The head to body ratio is a **part-part ratio**.

The head to height ratio is a **part-whole ratio**.

12. a. Explain what is meant by *part-part ratio* and *part-whole ratio*.

    b. Look back at the problems in this section about cars speeding and not-speeding. Describe a part-part ratio and a part-whole ratio fitting this situation.

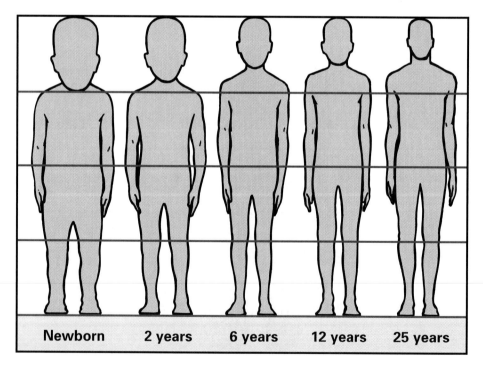

| Newborn | 2 years | 6 years | 12 years | 25 years |

The head-to-height ratio changes over a person's lifetime.

13. a. Use the chart above to estimate the head-to-height ratio of a newborn baby.

    b. What happens to the ratio as a person gets older? Explain.

Bottles (page 1)

1. Camp's juice cases contain 15 bottles of juice. Use the following ratio tables to find out how many bottles there are in different numbers of cases:

    a. 8 cases

Cases	1	2	4	8				
Bottles	15							

    b. 6 cases

Cases	1	2	3	6				
Bottles	15							

    c. 15 cases

Cases	1	10	5	15				
Bottles	15							

    d. 9 cases

Cases	1	10	9					
Bottles	15							

    e. 99 cases

Cases	1							
Bottles	15							

2. Jake wants 155 bottles of Camp's juice. Use the following ratio table to determine how many cases he needs to order. Add more columns if necessary.

Cases	1							
Bottles	15							

Bottles (page 2)

Camp's Beverages sells cases of mineral water and juice.
A full case of mineral water contains 12 bottles.

3. Fill in this ratio table to find out how many bottles
   there are in 24 cases. (You do not have to use all
   columns in the table. You may add more columns
   if you need them.)

Cases	1						
Bottles	12						

   Twenty-four cases of Camp's mineral water contain
   _____ bottles.

4. Use the ratio table to find out how many bottles there
   are in 31 cases.

   (You may add more columns if you need them. On
   the other hand, you may leave columns blank if you
   do not need them.)

Cases	1						
Bottles	12						

   Thirty-one cases of Camp's mineral water contain
   _____ bottles.

5. Jake wants 98 bottles of mineral water for an office
   party. How many cases will he order?

Cases	1						
Bottles	12						

   For Jake's order of 98 bottles, he will order _____
   cases of Camp's mineral water.

Key to Success

BRITANNICA
Mathematics
in
Context

Level 3

Lesson Ten Activities

Scale and Ratio

Scale Drawings

Tim wants to rearrange the furniture in his room. He decides to make a **scale drawing** of his room, called a **floor plan**. He can use the floor plan to try out different room arrangements. This will save him the work of moving the actual furniture. He can move the paper furniture on his scale drawing.

Tim's actual room dimensions are 2.6 m wide and 3 m long.

Tim decides to use graph paper. His first idea is to draw a floor plan with dimensions 26 cm by 30 cm.

1. **a.** Explain why you think Tim decided on these floor plan dimensions.

   b. Will his floor plan drawing fit on the graph paper on the next page? Why or why not?

   c. What dimensions would you use to draw the floor plan of Tim's room? Explain how you arrived at your answer.

Tim decides to use dimensions of 13 cm by 15 cm for his floor plan.

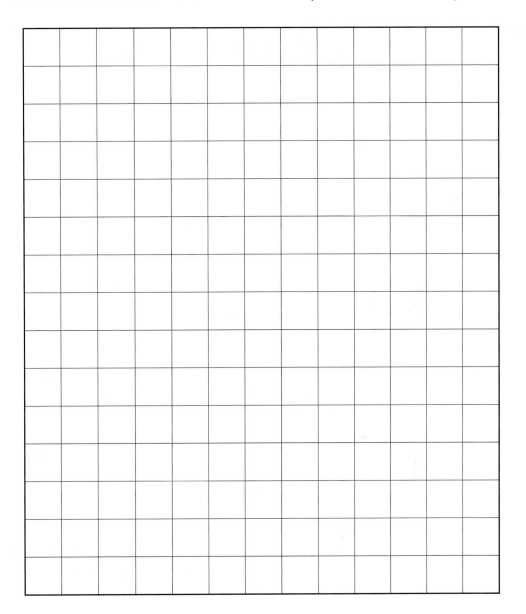

2. Use **Student Activity Sheet 1** to draw the same floor plan Tim will draw of his room. Indicate the location for the door to his room on the floor plan.

A **double number line** is a useful tool to show the relationship between the dimensions in a drawing and the actual room dimensions. Here is a double number line that belongs to the scale drawing of Tim's room.

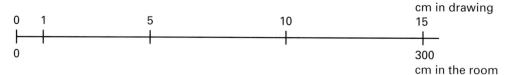

cm in drawing

| 0 | 1 | 5 | 10 | 15 |

0   300
                                                                cm in the room

3. Copy this double number line under your own scale drawing on **Student Activity Sheet 1** and fill in the missing numbers on the bottom of the line.

Activity

Here is the furniture for Tim's room.

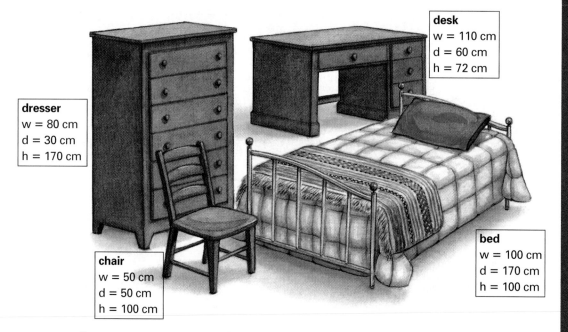

desk
w = 110 cm
d = 60 cm
h = 72 cm

dresser
w = 80 cm
d = 30 cm
h = 170 cm

chair
w = 50 cm
d = 50 cm
h = 100 cm

bed
w = 100 cm
d = 170 cm
h = 100 cm

On a separate piece of graph paper, draw each piece of furniture to the same scale as the floor plan. Each miniature piece of furniture should represent the space the actual furniture takes up on the floor of Tim's room. A double number line can be helpful to make your calculations.

4. Draw your favorite arrangement for Tim's room on your floor plan on **Student Activity Sheet 1**.

The double number line used for Tim's floor plan indicates a **scale ratio** of 1:20.

5. Reflect Look back at the double number line for Tim's floor plan. Describe how you would explain to someone what it means that Tim's floor plan has a scale ratio of 1:20.

Tim's older sister, Jenna, wants to rent an apartment. Below is a floor plan of an apartment she likes a lot. She wants to use the floor plan to find the dimensions of the living room.

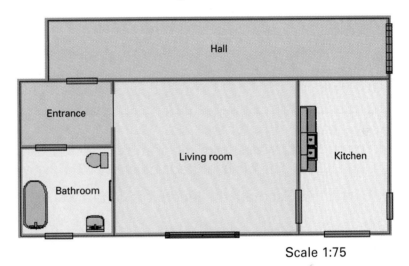

Scale 1:75

6. a. Use this ratio table to help Jenna find the length of the living room.

Length in Drawing (in cm)	1			
Actual Length (in cm)	75			

b. What is the actual width of the living room? Show your calculations.

Maps

You may remember doing other work with **scale lines** on a map. Scale lines are like a ruler. You can use scale lines to estimate or even measure distances on a map. The map below shows the northern part of San Francisco.

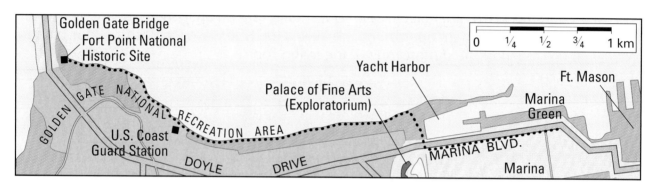

Sarita walks from the Marina Green to Fort Point National Historic Site. The black dotted line shows Sarita's walking path.

7. Estimate the length of Sarita's walking path.

If you want to find a distance on a map, you need to go from one measurement unit to another. The following conversions are common. Do you know them?

8. Check what you know by copying and filling in the following measuring relationships. Add others that you might know.

1 meter = ... centimeters

1 kilometer = ... meters

You can transform a scale line on the map into a double number line.

Here is a double number line adapted from the scale line on the San Francisco map.

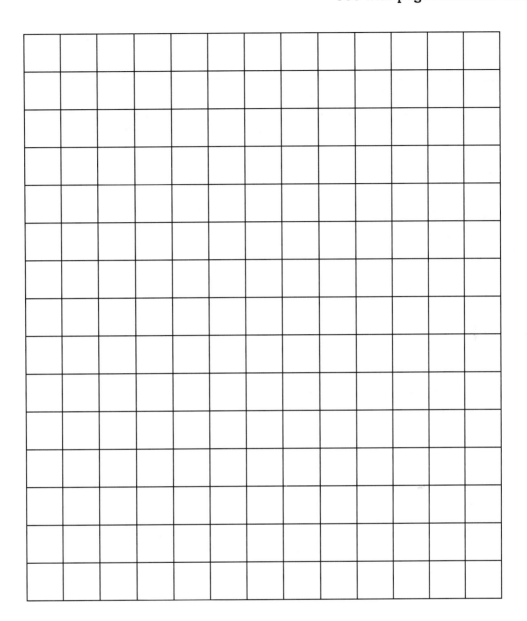

Tim decides to use dimensions of 13 cm by 15 cm for his floor plan.

2. Draw the same floor plan Tim will draw of his room. Indicate the
   location for the door to his room on the floor plan.

Double Number Line:

A double number line is a useful tool to show the relationship between the
dimensions in a drawing and the actual room dimensions. An example for
Tim's room is in your student book.

3. Copy the double number line under your scale drawing and fill in the
   missing numbers.

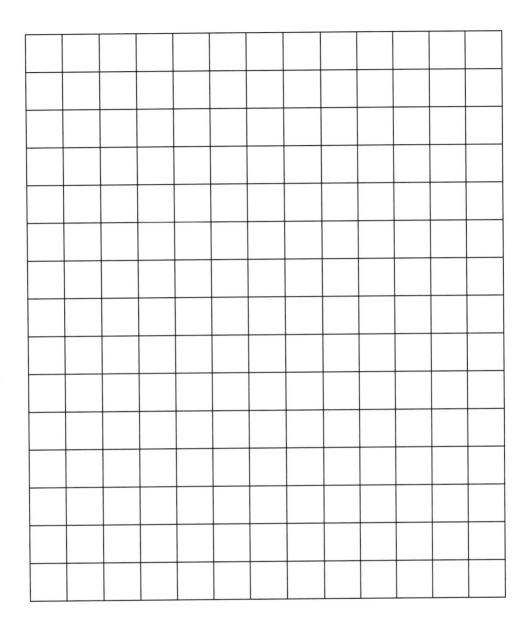

On a separate piece of graph paper, draw each piece of furniture to
the same scale as the floor plan. Each miniature piece of furniture
should represent the space the actual furniture takes up on the
floor of Tim's room. A double number line can be helpful to make
your calculations.

Scale (page 1)

To find the area of a space, it is important to write the dimension as a single unit, using either fractions or decimals.
For example, 7' 6" is $7\frac{1}{2}$' or 7.5'.

1. Write the dimensions of each room as a single unit.

   a. Bedroom   10' 3" × 16' 6"   _____

   b. Family Room   16' 9" × 15' 4"   _____

Here you see a drawing of the bedroom. Note that this drawing is not to scale.

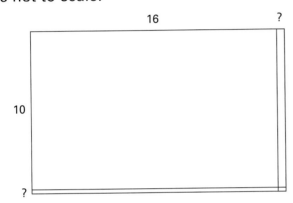

2. Fill in the missing numbers and calculate the area of the bedroom in square feet.

A common scale for working with floor plans is 1":48". So one inch in the drawing is 48 inches in reality.

3. Use the scale line to find the actual dimensions of this bathroom using inches.

Scale (page 2)

The scale 1″:48″ is often written as 1″:4′, and called a *quarter-inch scale*.

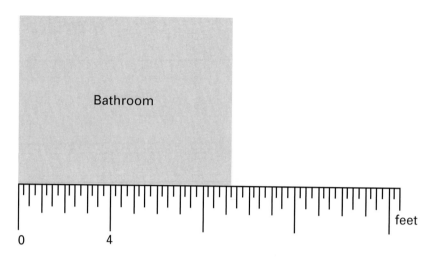

4. a. Use this scale line to find the actual dimensions of the bathroom using feet.

   b. How can you use both scale lines to find the dimensions of the bathroom using a whole number of feet and inches?

5. Make a scale drawing of the two rooms in problem 1 on a quarter-inch scale.

Key to Success

BRITANNICA
Mathematics
in
Context

Level 3

Lesson
Eleven
Activities

Using Formulas

Temperature

Kim has a pen pal in Bolivia named Lucrecia. Lucrecia is planning a visit to the United States, and she will stay with Kim's family.

Lucrecia sent this letter from Bolivia.

Dear Kim,

The weather has been beautiful. We have had a week with temperatures of about 25°C. On Wednesday, it was even 30°C. This is a bit too hot for me.

We went swimming in the lake. The water was not very warm, only 18°C, but it was great to cool off. It's hard to imagine that a week ago it was only around 16°C. I had to wear a sweater all day.

What is the weather like in your city? Do I have to bring a sweater? At home it cools down in the evenings. Last night we had a thunderstorm, and the temperature dropped by 10 degrees!

I look forward to seeing you.

Lucrecia

1. Estimate the temperatures in degrees **Fahrenheit** for the **Celsius** temperatures Lucrecia mentions in her letter.

The thermometer shows both Fahrenheit and Celsius temperatures.

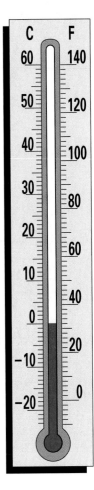

2. a. How can you use this thermometer to find the answers to problem 1?

    b. Check the estimates you made for problem 1. Were they close to what the thermometer tells you?

3. a. Look carefully at the thermometer. An increase of 10°C corresponds to an increase of how many °F?

    b. Use your answer to part **a** to answer the following question. An increase of 1°C corresponds to an increase of how many °F?

    c. Could you have answered part **b** just by looking at the thermometer? Explain.

When you use a thermometer to convert temperatures, you sometimes have to estimate the degrees because of the way the scale lines are drawn.

 4. **Reflect** Do you think it is possible to calculate a Fahrenheit temperature for each Celsius temperature? Why or why not?

Here is a formula, written different ways, for converting temperatures from degrees Celsius (C) into degrees Fahrenheit (F).

$$1.8 \times C + 32 = F$$
$$1.8C + 32 = F$$
$$F = 1.8C + 32$$

5. a. Explain where the numbers in the formula come from. (Hint: Use the thermometer and your answer for problem 3b.)

    b. Write the formula using an **arrow string**.

The formula and the thermometer tell you the relationship between *C* (the temperature in degrees Celsius) and *F* (the temperature in degrees Fahrenheit).

You can also make a graph to show the relationship.

6. a. First, fill in the table on the top of **Student Activity Sheet 1**. (Add some temperatures of your own choice, too.)

C	−20	−15	−10	−5	0	5		
F								

b. Describe any patterns you see in the table.

c. Graph the information from the table at the top of **Student Activity Sheet 1**. (Notice that *C* is on the horizontal axis and *F* is on the vertical axis.)

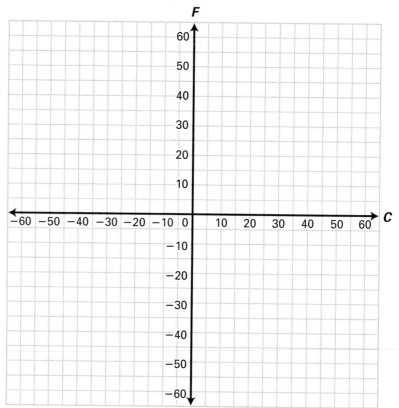

Your graph in problem 6 should be a straight line.

7. How could you tell that the graph would be a straight line?

8. There is only one temperature that has the same value in degrees Celsius and degrees Fahrenheit. What temperature is this? Describe how you found your answer.

To convert temperatures, you can use a thermometer, a graph, a table, or a formula. There are many ways to write a formula that converts between Fahrenheit and Celsius.

9. a. Write a **reverse arrow string** to convert temperatures from Fahrenheit to Celsius. (Hint: Use the answer to problem 5b.)

   b. Write a formula that converts temperatures from Fahrenheit to Celsius.

Most formulas for converting between the two types of degrees are not easy to use if you are trying to do the calculation mentally. Sometimes people use estimation formulas for converting in their heads. Here is an estimation formula to change Celsius to Fahrenheit.

Double the Celsius value and add 30.

10. Make up an estimation formula to convert Fahrenheit to Celsius. The freezing point of water is 0° in Celsius and 32° in Fahrenheit. Check your formula, using the temperatures for freezing.

11. a. Convert two temperatures from Celsius to Fahrenheit and two temperatures from Fahrenheit to Celsius, using the estimation formulas.

   b. Do the same using the direct formulas.

   c. **Reflect** Compare the results. Why would people use estimation formulas if the results are not very accurate?

Dale remembered a rule he learned in school last year for converting temperatures. He uses an arrow string to write it on the chalkboard.

$$\xrightarrow{+\ 40} \quad \xrightarrow{\times\ 1.8} \quad \xrightarrow{-\ 40}$$

Kim wonders if this rule could be correct. She says: "First you add 40, and then you subtract 40, so nothing happens. You can skip those two arrows."

12. a. Do you agree with Kim? Why or why not?

   b. Does Dale's rule work?

6. a. Fill in the table. (Add some temperatures of your own choice, too.)

   b. Describe any patterns you see in the table.

   c. Graph the information from the table. (Notice that *C* is on the horizontal axis and F is on the vertical axis.)

C	−20	−15	−10	−5	0	5		
F								

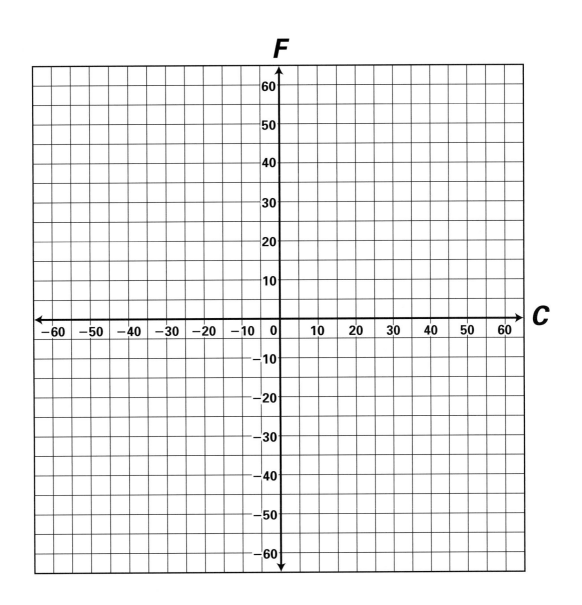

With and Without a Calculator

1. Use your calculator to find the cost of the following items.
   Note that stores round up all prices to the nearest cent.

   a. 1.365 kilograms of pears at $3.10 per kilogram

   b. 0.723 kg of broccoli at $3.25 per kilogram

   c. 1.739 kg of collard greens at $1.79 per kilogram

   d. 1.396 kg of strawberries at $1.65 per kilogram

   e. 0.842 kg of oranges at $2.98 per kilogram

Michelle is supposed to use her calculator to do her homework, but
the decimal point key is broken. To calculate the price of 1.293 kg
of spinach that costs $2.98 per kilogram, Michelle enters 1293 × 298,
and her calculator displays 385314. She can then figure out where to
place the decimal point by estimating the correct answer.

2. Without using your calculator, find the answer to 1.293 × $2.98.
   Explain your strategy.

3. Without using your calculator, help Michelle find the correct
   price for each of the following items.

   a. 3.129 kg of grapes, selling for $3.10 per kilogram
      (Michelle's calculator displays 969990.)

   b. 21.38 kg of apples, selling for $1.26 per kilogram
      (Michelle's calculator displays 269388)

   c. 0.729 kg of lemons, selling for $4.10 per kilogram
      (Michelle's calculator displays 298890.)

   d. 3.28 kg of oranges, selling for $4.98 per kilogram
      (Michelle's calculator displays 163344.)

   e. 0.083 kg of parsley, selling for $5.50 per kilogram
      (Michelle's calculator displays 45650).

Estimations

Animations

To make an animation, you need many pictures to show movement. Hand-drawn animations need 12 frames per second.

1. Estimate how many pictures you will need to draw for a 5-minute cartoon.

Leaking Faucet

Each second, two drops drip from this leaking faucet.

It takes 20 drops to fill one cubic centimeter. Recall that 1 liter fits exactly into one cubic decimeter. Pete's father puts a 10-liter bucket under the tap to catch the water.

2. Will this bucket be large enough to catch all the water during the night, from 8 P.M. till 8 A.M.? Justify your opinion.

New York Marathon

About 30,000 runners sign up to run in the annual New York Marathon.

3. Estimate how long the line of 30,000 participating runners might be. Show your assumptions.

4. A reporter at the race stated that more than two million spectators stood along the route. Does this number make sense? Show your reasoning.

Key to Success

BRITANNICA
Mathematics
in
Context

Level 3

Lesson
Twelve
Activities

More Formulas

Building Stairs

The picture shows a staircase.
All of the steps are the same size.
Each step has two main parts:
the *riser* and the *tread*.

The vertical measure, or the height,
of a step is called the **rise** (*R*).

The horizontal measure, or depth,
of a step is called the **tread** (*T*).

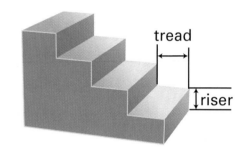

Activity

You are going to use stiff paper to build
a model staircase like the one shown.

- In the center of a piece of stiff
  paper, draw a rectangle that is
  exactly 20 centimeters (cm) long
  and 10 cm wide. Label the corners
  of the rectangle A, B, C, and D as
  shown in the diagram.

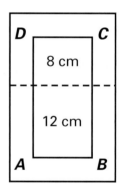

- Across your paper, draw a dotted
  line that is 8 cm below the top of
  the rectangle.

- Fill the rectangle with lines that are
  alternately 3 cm and 2 cm apart,
  as shown in the next diagram.
  (It is easy to keep your lines parallel,
  using a ruler and a triangle.)

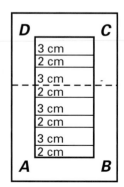

- Fold the paper along the dotted line and cut along the long sides of the rectangle. Do not cut along the short sides.

- Fold the solid lines like an accordion so that you end up with a staircase. The first fold should be on side *DC* folded toward you (out). Fold the next line away from you (in). Continue alternating the fold direction until the staircase is finished.

You now have a model staircase.

- Label the wall and the floor on your model as shown.

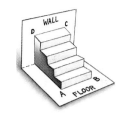

The stairs you made fit nicely with the floor and the wall. In other words, the treads and the floor are perfectly horizontal and the risers and the wall are perfectly vertical.

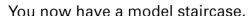

1. **Reflect** Do you think this is a coincidence, or were they designed that way? Why do you think so?

2. **a.** Measure and record the height and depth of the whole staircase (depth is measured along the floor).

   b. What are the values for *T* and *R* in the steps you made?

   c. How are the height and depth of the whole staircase related to the rise and tread of each step? Explain.

3. On your model staircase, make the fold between the floor and the wall in a different place. Is the tread of each step in your model still perfectly horizontal? Is the rise of each step exactly vertical? Explain why or why not.

4. **a.** Would the designs shown here make good staircases? Explain.

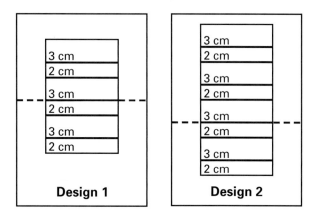

Design 1 **Design 2**

b. Copy the drawing below into your notebook. Draw a fold line where it will create a good model staircase.

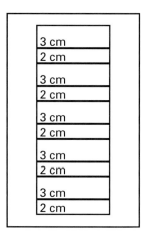

c. Reflect What are some rules for making good model staircases?

Not all stairs are easy to climb.

5. Order the staircases shown below according to how easy you think they would be to climb. Give reasons to support your choices.

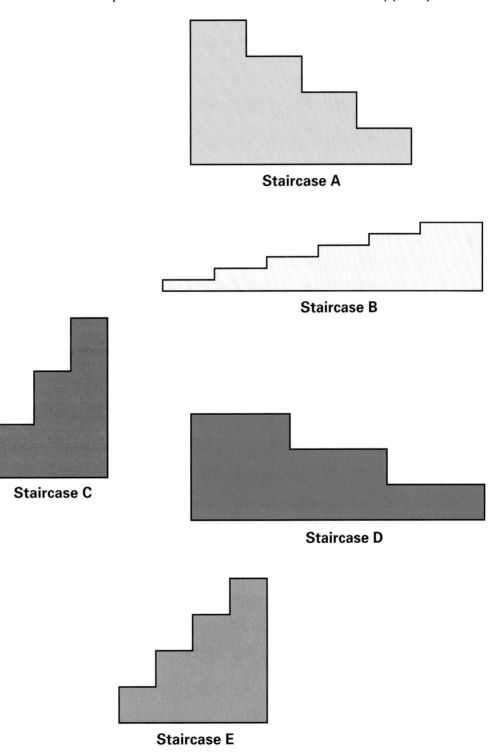

Staircase A

Staircase B

Staircase C

Staircase D

Staircase E

For problem 5, you may have listed the steepness of the stairs as one factor that affects how easy they are to climb.

6. What are some advantages and disadvantages of steep stairs?

If you are not careful about choosing the measurements for the rise and tread of a set of stairs, you can end up with stairs that are difficult to climb.

7. What could you do to make the stairs steeper?

Stairs that are easy to climb usually fit the following rule:

$$2 \times Rise + Tread = Length\ of\ one\ pace$$
or
$$2R + T = P$$

An adult's **pace** is about 63 cm. So the rule can be written as follows:

$$2R + T = 63$$

8. a. A contractor wants to build a set of stairs with a rise of 19 cm for each step. What size will the tread be if she follows the rule? Explain.

b. For another set of stairs, the contractor knows that the tread must be 23 cm. How high will each rise be if the contractor uses the rule? Explain.

You have now found two combinations of rise and tread measurements that fit the rule based on an adult pace of 63 cm.

9. a. Find a few more pairs of numbers that fit the rule.

b. On **Student Activity Sheet 1**, graph all of the pairs of rise and tread measurements that fit the rule.

You can make stairs that are difficult to climb even when you use the formula.

10. Which points on the graph would represent stairs that are difficult to climb?

11. What happens to the tread (T) if you add 1 cm to the rise (R) and are using the rule? Can you see this on your graph?

12. Using the rule, when do *R* and *T* have the same value?

Here is another rule that helps in designing stairs that are easy to climb.

Rise ≤ 20 cm

This means that the rise is less than or equal to 20 cm.

13. a. Why would this rule make stairs easier to climb?

    b. Find a way to show this rule on your graph.

    c. Find measurements for some stairs that fit both rules.

    d. There are some situations that do not allow for stairs that are easy to climb. What could be some reasons for having stairs that are not easy to climb?

Think about the dimensions of the paper stairs you made earlier. Suppose the paper stairs are a model that uses the rule $2R + T = 63$ cm for an actual set of stairs.

14. a. What are the measurements for the rise and tread in the actual flight of stairs?

    b. What are the height and depth measurements of the whole flight of stairs?

Here are some other rules used for building stairs in different kinds of buildings.

Private Homes
Rise—maximum 20 cm
Tread—minimum 23 cm

Public Buildings
Rise—maximum 18 cm
Tread—minimum 28 cm

15. a. Why do you think that there is a maximum for the rise?

    b. Why is there a minimum for the tread and not a maximum?

Rise (in cm)

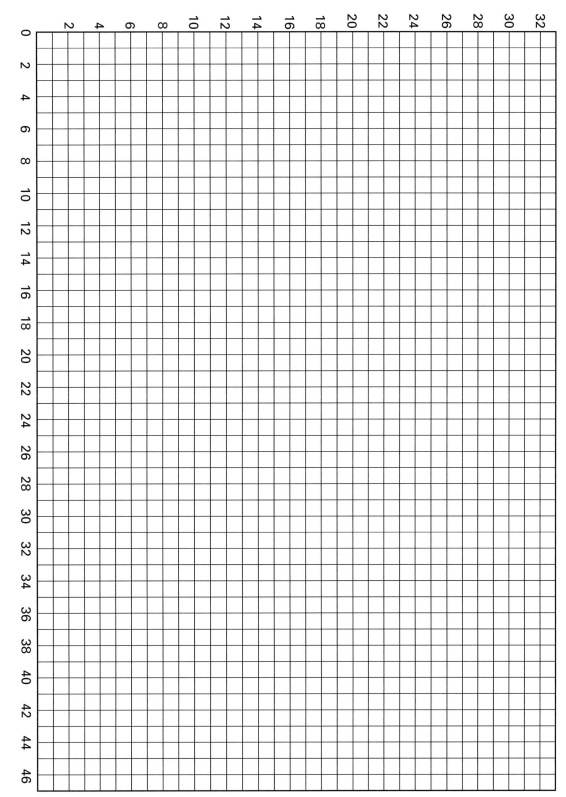

Tread (in cm)

The Green Air factory makes refrigerators.

A serial number is etched into each refrigerator in sequential order. Here are the serial numbers of the first three refrigerators made last Tuesday.

SR–341–05–0193

SR–341–05–0194

SR–341–05–0195

1. List the last four digits of the serial numbers of the next three refrigerators made at the Green Air factory.

Here are the serial numbers of the last three refrigerators made last Tuesday.

SR–341–05–3601

SR–341–05–3602

SR–341–05–3603

2. How many refrigerators were made last Tuesday?

Last Wednesday, the serial number SR–341–05–3604 was etched into the first refrigerator made, and the last refrigerator made had the serial number SR–341–05–7702.

3. How many refrigerators were made last Wednesday?

The last refrigerator made on Thursday had the serial number SR–341–05–9871, and the last refrigerator made on Friday had the serial number SR–341–06–3004.

4. How many refrigerators were made on Thursday? And on Friday?

Bar Code

Almost all products sold today have a bar code. For retail items, the bar code has a length of 13 digits. It shows information about the county of origin, the manufacturer, and the product. The last digit is a safeguard to check the other twelve digits.

This barcode has only twelve digits; it is missing the safeguard digit.

1122334455bb?

1. Carry out these calculations to find the missing last digit.

   Step 1 Starting from the left, add all digits in the odd position.

   Step 2 Multiply the result by 3.

   Step 3 Add all digits in the even position.

   Step 4 Add the results of Step 2 and Step 3.

   Step 5 Determine what number needs to be added to the result of Step 4 to make it divisible by 10.

Here is a different barcode.

0 1 2 3 4 5 6   7 8 9 0 0 5

2. Verify that this bar code has a correct safeguard digit.

Here is a copy of the barcode for a new book.

3. Find the correct safeguard digit for this book.

Key to Success

BRITANNICA
Mathematics
in
Context

Level 3

Lesson Thirteen Activities

Formulas and Geometry

Lichens

Many formulas are used in geometry. In this section, you will revisit some of the formulas you studied earlier for finding the area and volume of different shapes and solids.

A lichen (pronounced LIKE-en) is a type of fungus that grows on rocks, on walls, on trees, and in the tundra. Lichens are virtually indestructible. No place is too hot, too cold, or too dry for them to live.

Scientists can use lichens to estimate when glaciers disappeared. Lichens are always the first to move into new areas. So as the glacier recedes, lichens will appear very soon. The scientists know how fast lichens grow, so they use the area covered by the lichens to calculate how long ago a glacier disappeared.

Many lichens grow more or less in the shape of a circle.

1. Estimate the **area** covered by this lichen in square centimeters (cm^2).

You can use a circle as a model for the area covered by a lichen. Remember that the formula to find the area of a circle is:

$$Area = \pi \times radius \times radius$$

or

$$Area = \pi r^2$$

Your calculator may have a π key. If it doesn't, use 3.14 as an approximation for π.

2. a. Make a drawing of a circle with a radius of 2 cm. Use a compass!

   b. What is the diameter of your circle?

The formula $Area = \pi r^2$ can be written as an arrow string.

$$r \xrightarrow{\ square\ } \ldots\ldots \xrightarrow{\ \times\ \pi\ } area$$

3. Use the formula or the arrow string to find the area of the circle from problem 2. Round your answer to the nearest tenth and be sure to include the unit measurement.

The diameter of the lichen shown on page 134 is about 1 cm.

4. a. What is the radius of a circle with a diameter of 1 cm?

   b. Use the formula or the arrow string to find the area of the circle. Round your answer to the nearest tenth and be sure to include the unit measurement.

   c. Was your estimation of the area covered by the lichen close?

The table shows the relationship between the radius of a circle and its area.

Radius (in cm)	0	0.5	1	1.5	2	2.5	3	4
Area (in cm²)	0		3.1					

5. a. Copy the table in your notebook and fill in the empty spaces.

   b. Use graph paper to draw a graph to represent this relationship.

   c. Describe the graph. Does it seem to be a straight line? Explain how you can tell.

A scientific article reported that a lichen on a glacier covered 34 cm².

6. If you knew the radius, you could figure out how wide the lichen in the report was. How could you find an estimate for the radius?

7. a. Sammi says the radius would be 17 cm because 134 divided by 2 is 17. What do you think of Sammi's idea?

   b. Sammi insists that his idea is a good one. Think of some examples of areas that would either support his idea or show that it is wrong.

   c. Jorge has a different idea. He says that because the formula for the area uses square numbers, you can "unsquare" the number. What do you think of Jorge's idea?

To "unsquare" a number, mathematicians use the symbol $\sqrt{}$. It is usually read as *taking the* **square root** *of* instead of **unsquaring**.

8. Find the square root of each of the following numbers. Why don't you need a calculator to do so?

   a. 25   **b.** 64   **c.** 121   **d.** $\frac{1}{4}$

9. **a.** Use the $\sqrt{}$ key on your calculator to find the square root of 150.

   b. Write on a sheet of paper the answer your calculator gives you for $\sqrt{150}$. Clear the calculator and calculate the square of this number. If there is a difference, can you explain the difference between this number and the answer you got in part **a**?

For most numbers, it is not possible to find the exact square root because there are an infinite number of decimal places, and the decimals never form a repeating pattern. The only time you get an exact answer is when you start with a square number like 49 or $6\frac{1}{4}$.

10. What does the calculator do since it cannot show a decimal that keeps going?

Here is an arrow string that makes use of square numbers.

$$number \xrightarrow{\text{square}} \ldots\ldots \xrightarrow{\times\,3} answer$$

11. **a.** What is the *answer* if the *number* is 5? If the *number* is 10? If the *number* is $\frac{2}{3}$?

   b. Reverse the arrow string. Use the $\sqrt{}$ sign.

   c. Find the *number* for each of the answers: 12, 24, and $\frac{3}{5}$.

   d. Make an arrow string using squares and roots. Find two *numbers* and two *answers* and have them checked by a classmate.

Here is the arrow string for the area of a circle.

$$r \xrightarrow{\text{square}} \ldots\ldots \xrightarrow{\times\,\pi} area$$

12. **a.** Reverse the arrow string for the area of a circle.

   b. Use the reverse arrow string to find a formula for the radius of a circle if you know its area.

   c. Use the reverse arrow string or the formula to find the radius of a circle with an area of 35 cm². Give your answer to one decimal place.

Track Your Time and Accuracy (page 1)

Do each problem as quickly as you can.

Record your Start Time: [ ]

1. a. $10 \times 28 =$

   b. $5 \times 28 =$

2. a. $2 \times 5 \times 7 =$

   b. $2 \times 18 \times 5 =$

3. a. $10 \times 30 =$

   b. $20 \times 30 =$

4. a. $10 \times 3.1 =$

   b. $100 \times 3.1 =$

5. a. $3 \times 30 =$

   b. $6 \times 15 =$

6. a. $10 \times 15 =$

   b. $11 \times 15 =$

7. a. $10 \times 25 =$

   b. $9 \times 25 =$

8. a. $40 \div 10 =$

   b. $4 \div 10 =$

9. a. $6 \times 15 =$

   b. $8 \times 45 =$

10. a. $1.2 \times \underline{\quad} = 12$

    b. $1.2 \times \underline{\quad} = 6$

Record Your Finish Time: [ ]

Fill in your results. Keep track of your results.
With practice, you will improve both your speed and accuracy.

My Results:

Total Time

_____

Total Correct

_____

Track Your Time and Accuracy (page 2)

Do each problem as quickly as you can.

Record your Start Time:

1. a. 10 × 23 =   **6. a.** 10 × 25 =

   b. 20 × 23 =   **b.** 11 × 25 =

2. a. 4 × 60 =   **7. a.** 10 × 15 =

   b. 8 × 60 =   **b.** 9 × 15 =

3. a. 10 × 21 =   **8. a.** 60 ÷ 10 =

   b. 20 × 21 =   **b.** 6 ÷ 10 =

4. a. 2 × 5 × 9 =   **9. a.** 6 × 25 =

   b. 2 × 17 × 5 =   **b.** 8 × 35 =

5. a. 10 × 5.2 =   **10. a.** 1.4 × ____ = 14

   b. 100 × 5.2 =   **b.** 1.4 × ____ = 7

Record your Finish Time:

Fill in your results. Keep track of your results.
With practice, you will improve both your speed
and accuracy.

My Results:

Total Time

_____

Total Correct

_____

Key to Success

BRITANNICA
Mathematics
in
Context

Level 3

Lesson Fourteen Activities

More Formulas and Geometry

Circles and Solids

Valerie wants to make a mold she can later use to make candles. She decides to use a cylinder-shaped mold. For the base of the mold, she has cut a circle that has a 6-cm diameter.

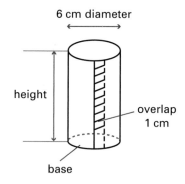

1. **a.** Make an accurate drawing of a circle that is 6 cm in diameter. Use a compass.

   b. Use a strip of paper to find the size of the mantle of the mold. Allow at least 1 cm overlap to glue the mantle together. What are the measurements of the mantle without the overlap?

   Valerie used this formula for the mantle of her mold:

   circumference of a circle = π × diameter

   c. Explain why this formula makes sense.

   Fruit drinks come in cans of different sizes. Some cans are narrow and tall; others are wide and short.

2. **a.** What shapes are juice cans usually?

   b. Is it possible for cans in different shapes to contain the same amount of liquid?

This juice can is made up of two circles and a rectangle.

The can shown in the drawing has a height of 15 cm. The diameter of the bottom is 7 cm.

3. a. Calculate the area of the bottom of the can.

   b. Calculate the **volume** of the can. Remember that the formula for the volume of any cylinder is:

   $$Volume = area\ of\ Base \times Height$$

   c. What are the measurements of the rectangle that makes the sides of the can?

   d. The can is made of tin. How much tin (in cm²) is needed to make this can?

This type of fruit juice is also available in cans that are twice as high.

4. a. Compare the amounts of fruit juice that each can contains.

   b. How do the **surface areas** of the cans compare? Be prepared to explain your answer without making calculations.

5. Suppose one can has double the diameter of another can.

   a. Do you think the amount of liquid that fits in the larger can will double? Give mathematical reasons to support your answer.

   b. What can you tell about the surface area of the larger can compared to that of the original can?

Pyramids

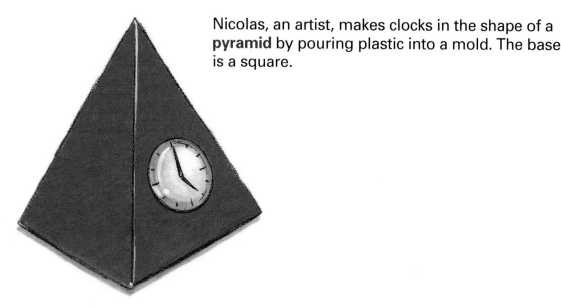

Nicolas, an artist, makes clocks in the shape of a **pyramid** by pouring plastic into a mold. The base is a square.

Remember that the formula for the volume of any pyramid is:

$$Volume = \tfrac{1}{3} \times area\ of\ Base \times Height$$

This formula can be rewritten as:

$$Volume = \tfrac{1}{3}\, a^2 h$$

(a is the length of one side of the base; h is the height)

6. Explain why this formula can be used to calculate the volume of a pyramid.

7. Write the formula as an arrow string.

Matthew made this arrow string:

$$a \xrightarrow{\times \frac{1}{3}} \dots \xrightarrow{square} \dots \xrightarrow{\times h} Volume$$

8. Matthew made a mistake. What was his mistake?

Nicolas wants to know how much plastic is needed for 250 of the clock pyramids. The square measures 2 dm by 2 dm, and the height is $1\tfrac{1}{2}$ dm.

9. How many cubic decimeters (dm³) of plastic are needed?

Nicolas thinks the clock pyramids should be a little larger so they will fit in the gift boxes he can buy. He wants the new pyramids to have a volume of $2\frac{1}{2}$ dm³ each.

10. **a.** Write the reverse arrow string to find the area of the base of the new pyramid.

b. Find the length of the square that is the base of the pyramid.

c. To how many decimal places did you round your answer for part **b**? Explain why you think what you did is reasonable.

Name _____ Date _____ Class_____

Units (page 1)

Here are two different rulers. One is marked with inches and the other with centimeters.

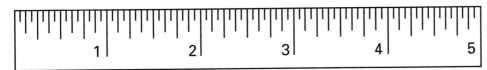

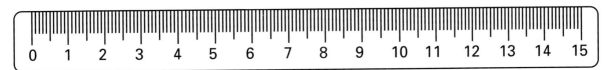

1. a. Which ruler—the first or the second—shows centimeters? How do you know?

  b. Both the centimeter and inch are partitioned into smaller units. Compare and contrast these partitions. Which one is based on units of ten?

2. You may use the two rulers to complete:

  a. one inch is about _____ centimeters.

  b. one centimeter is about _____ inch.

3. How long is one meter? Look around you. Is there anything in the classroom that is about one meter long or wide or high?

4. Compare a meter stick with a yardstick. Which one is based on units of ten?

5. Leo states that a meter is approximately 10% longer than a yard. Is he right? Explain.

A centimeter (cm) is one-hundredth of a meter (m).

There are two different ways to describe this relationship, with a fraction and with a decimal.

   $1 \text{ cm} = \frac{1}{100} \text{ m}$ $1 \text{ cm} = 0.01 \text{ m}$

6. Describe each of the following relationships in two ways, with a fraction and with a decimal.

Fraction	**Decimal**
a. 2 cm = _____ m	2 cm = _____ m
b. __ cm = $\frac{1}{2}$ m	__ cm = _____ m
c. 25 cm = _____ m	25 cm = _____ m
d. 7.5 cm = _____ m	7.5 cm = _____ m

MiC Key to Success Level 3

Units (page 2)

The height of this MP3 player is one decimeter.

This height is drawn in its actual size.

7. a. How many centimeters is this?

    b. How many decimeters are in one meter?

8. Use two different ways to describe the relationship between a decimeter and a meter, with a fraction and with a decimal.

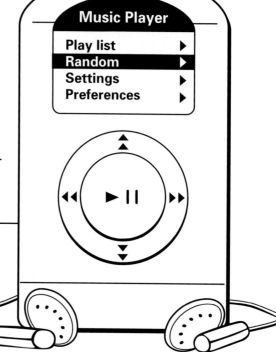

Millimeters, centimeters, decimeters, and **meters** are metric units used to measure length.

The prefixes, *deci*, *centi*, and *milli*, are derived from Latin.

Deci means one-tenth.
One decimeter (dm) is one-tenth of a meter (m).

Centi means one-hundredth.
One centimeter (cm) is one-hundredth of a meter.

Milli means one-thousandth.
One millimeter (mm) is one-thousandth of a meter.

9. Describe each of the following relationships in two ways, with a fraction and with a decimal.

	Fraction		**Decimal**
a. 1 mm	= _____ m	1 mm	= _____ m
b. 1 mm	= _____ cm	1 mm	= _____ cm
c. 3 dm	= _____ m	3 dm	= _____ m
d. 2.5 cm	= _____ dm	2.5 cm	= _____ dm
e. 7.5 mm	= _____ cm	7.5 mm	= _____ cm

Key to Success

BRITANNICA
Mathematics
in
Context

Level 3

Lesson
Fifteen
Activities

Problem Solving

Heavy Training

Your heart rate when you are lying or sitting is considered your normal or **resting heart rate**. When you fall asleep your heart rate slows, and when you exercise or are upset, your heart rate increases.

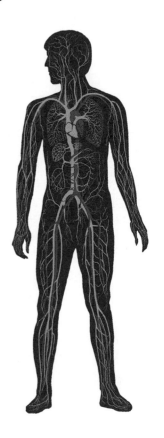

Activity

With a partner, find your resting heart rate. To do this, find your pulse in your neck or wrist and count the beats for 20 seconds. Your partner should watch the clock and tell you when to start counting and when to stop.

Heart rate is usually reported in terms of **beats per minute** (bpm). Use the pulse that you counted in 20 seconds to find your resting heart rate in beats per minute.

Switch roles with your partner and repeat the above procedure so that both of you know your resting heart rates.

Athletes who take part in endurance sports need to be in very good condition. When they compete, their heart rates increase.

Because it is dangerous for a person's heart rate to be too high for too long, athletes train specifically to increase their endurance. It is important for athletes to determine their **maximum heart rate**.

Finding the exact value of an athlete's maximum heart rate is difficult. There is, however, a rule that gives a close approximation.

> Subtract your age (A) in years from 220 to find your maximum heart rate (M) in beats per minute.

1. a. Write this rule as a formula.

   b. How does your resting heart rate compare to the maximum heart rate you calculated from the formula?

2. Make a graph on **Student Activity Sheet 1** that could be placed in a gym to help people find their maximum heart rates.

> **Warning:** The M value can vary with your physical condition. You should not use the above formula to gauge your own workouts without consulting a physician.

Use the formula and the graph you made for problem 2 to answer the following questions.

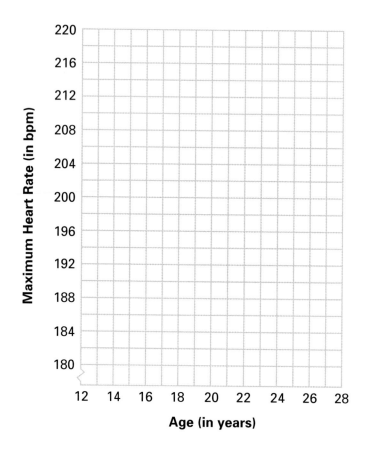

3. **a.** Who has a higher maximum heart rate: you or a teacher? Explain.

   b. What can you say about the relationship between age and maximum heart rate?

4. **a.** What is the highest possible maximum heart rate according to the formula? The lowest?

   b. Do you think this rule applies for people of any age? Explain.

Jacob is the trainer for John, Anita, and Carmen. He decides that these athletes should be using 75% of their maximum heart rate during their workouts. This heart rate is called the **training value** (T).

5. **a.** Write 75% as a fraction.

   b. Use the formula $M = 220 - A$ to create a new formula for the relationship between the training value T and age A.

Egyptian Art

The ancient Egyptians were fascinated by **proportions**. When they made drawings or sculptures of people, the measurements followed a set of rules. These rules help modern archaeologists reconstruct Egyptian pictures that have been damaged. Archaeologists have written these rules as formulas that are easy to use. The formulas are written in terms of the height of parts of the body from the ground.

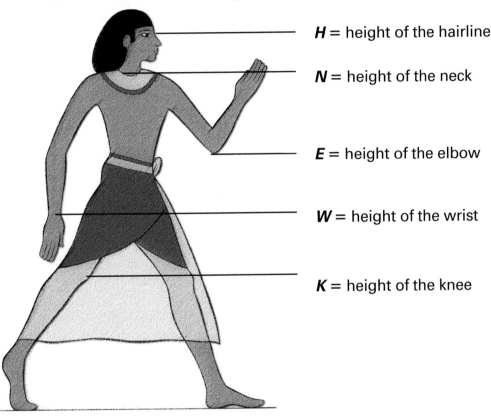

H = height of the hairline

N = height of the neck

E = height of the elbow

W = height of the wrist

K = height of the knee

These are the formulas used to figure out the proportions (each measurement is from the ground up):

$$H = 3K \qquad E - W = W - K$$
$$E = 2K \qquad N = \tfrac{8}{9} H$$

6. **a.** Translate the formula $E = 2K$ into an English sentence about the drawing.

   b. Describe how you can check whether $E - W$ equals $W - K$ in the drawing.

   c. Show whether the measurements of the Egyptian in the picture fit the given formulas.

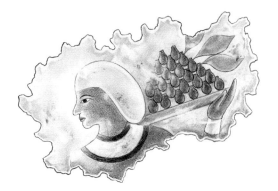

On a recent excavation, archaeologists discovered pieces of an ancient Egyptian drawing.

Unfortunately, parts of the drawing were missing. The archaeologists made careful tracings of the pieces they found.

7. Use **Student Activity Sheet 2** to reconstruct the original drawing.

   • First cut out the tracings that the archaeologists made.

   • Use the formulas to place each piece correctly. (Keep track of your calculations so that you can explain your process to someone else.) Glue the pieces onto a sheet of paper.

   • Then sketch the missing portions.

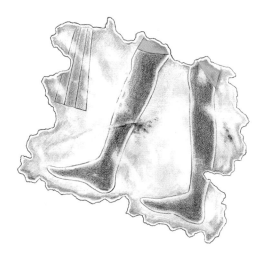

Later, while excavating the site, the team of archaeologists found fragments of another drawing. This drawing had grid lines over it, which the ancient Egyptians may have used to check the proportions. The archaeologists thought that this drawing would be easier to reconstruct than the first one because of the lines. After they looked at the pieces, however, they realized that it would be harder.

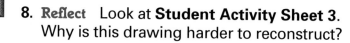

8. **Reflect** Look at **Student Activity Sheet 3**. Why is this drawing harder to reconstruct?

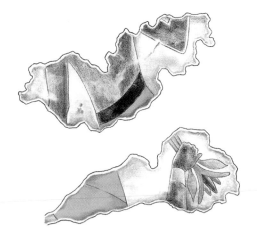

After looking carefully at the formulas, the archaeologists found a way to get around the problem.

9. Use **Student Activity Sheet 3** to reconstruct this picture. Cut out the pieces, glue them into the correct positions, and sketch the missing parts. (Remember to keep track of your calculations.)

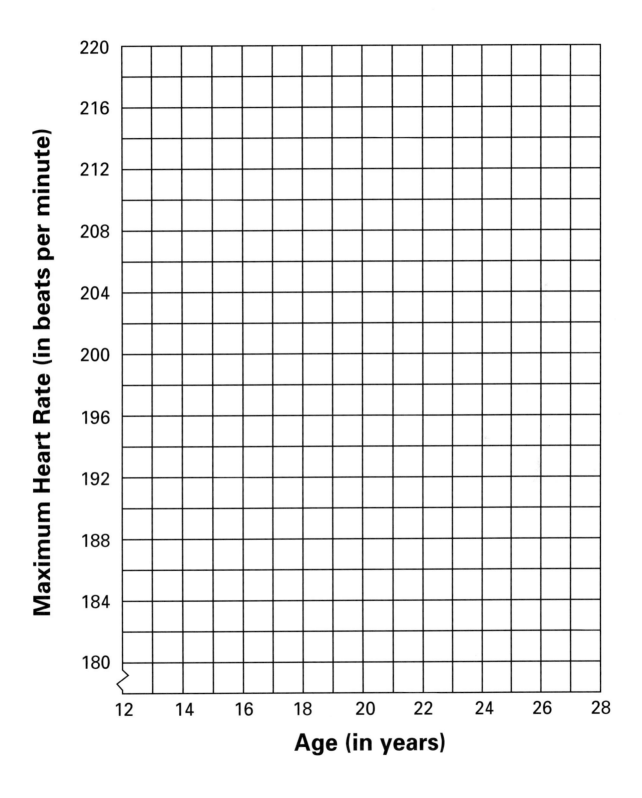

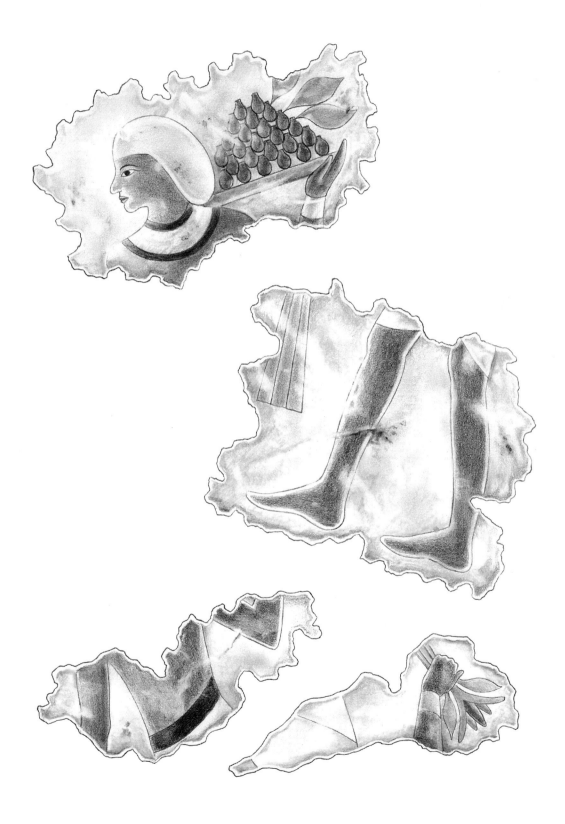

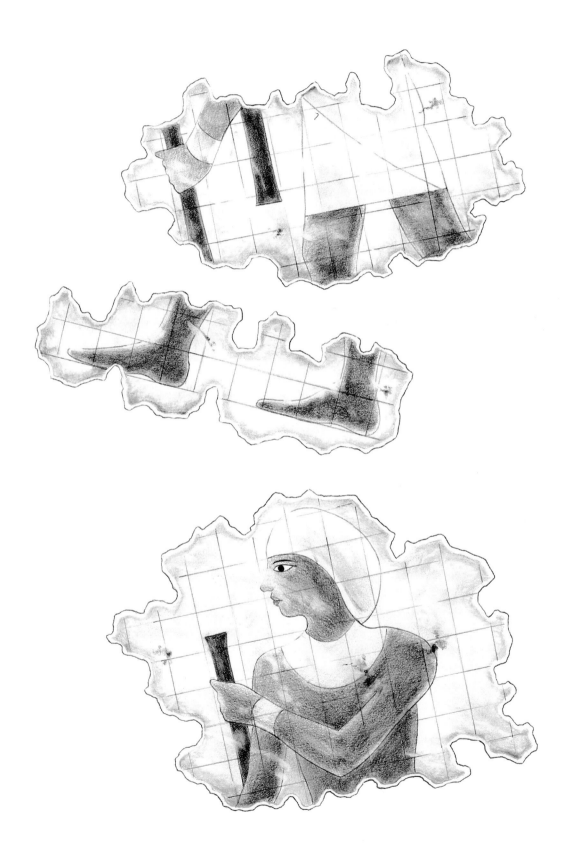

Key to Success

There are three base units in the metric system; the meter for length, the gram for weight or mass, and the liter for volume or capacity.

Multiples and fractions of these units are created by adding prefixes to the names of the defined units. For example, the prefix **kilo** means one thousand, so 1 **kilo**meter is 1,000 meters.

Prefix	Symbol	Meaning		
		as a Number	as a Power of Ten	in Words
Tera-	T-			Trillion
Giga-	G-			Billion
Mega-	M-			Million
Kilo-	k-			Thousand
Hecto-	h-	100	10^2	Hundred
Deca-	da-	10	10^1	Ten
Base Unit:				**Measures:**
Meter	m	1	10^0	Length
Gram	g	1		Weight
Liter	l	1		Volume
Deci-	d-	0.1	10^{-1}	Tenth
Centi-	c-	0.01		Hundredth
Milli-	m-	0.001		Thousandth
Micro-	μ-			Millionth
Nano-	n-			Billionth
Pico-	p-			Trillionth

1. Write five measurement units that have one of these prefixes and explain how it compares to its basic unit of meter, gram, or liter.

2. Write each prefix as a number by filling in the third column.

3. **a.** Write each prefix as a power of ten by filling in the fourth column.

   b. What pattern do you notice in the fourth column, Meaning as a Power of Ten?

Metric System (page 2)

4. Fill in the correct prefix, written out fully and abbreviated.

a. My pencil is about 150 _____ meters (___ m).

b. The circumference of the earth is about 40,000 _____ meters (___ m).

c. A hair grows approximately 0.3 _____ meters (___ m) a day.

d. A door height is about 200 _____ meters (___ m).

Five decimeters is five-tenths of a meter. Here are three ways to write this relationship.

5 dm = $\frac{5}{10}$ meter, as a fraction;

5 dm = 0.5 meter, as a decimal; and

5 dm = 5 × 10^{-1} meter, as a product of a number and a power of 10.

5. Describe each of the following relationships in three ways: as a fraction, as a decimal, and as a product of a number and a power of ten.

	Fraction	Decimal	Product (# × 10)
a. 5 cm			
b. 7 dm			
c. 15 mm			

You can see how small a millimeter is by looking at a centimeter ruler. How small is a micrometer?

6. Do you think you can see something of the size of one micrometer (μm)? Explain why or why not.

The size of a virus is between 0.02 and 0.25 μm.

7. Convert these measures to millimeters.

Nanotechnology is a branch of engineering that develops and uses devices that have sizes of only a few nanometers. Nanotechnology is sometimes called molecular manufacturing.

8. What fraction of a millimeter is one nanometer?

Key to Success

BRITANNICA
Mathematics
in
Context

Level 3

Lesson
Sixteen
Activities

Investigating Algorithms

Multiplication

Your neighbor offers to pay you to be his son's math tutor. You agree and set up your first tutoring session with Harvey.

Harvey comes over to your house, flops down in a chair, and opens his 4th grade math book to read this problem.

- A crate of Lemon Drop lemonade contains 24 bottles.

- If a supermarket manager bought 49 full crates, how many bottles did she buy?

You ask Harvey to try the problem, and he reluctantly picks up his pencil to begin solving it. As he works, you do the problem in your head.

1. a. Describe a way to estimate the answer.

   b. Adjust your estimate to find an exact answer.

Harvey uses a **ratio table** to do the problem.

Crates	1	10	5	4	9	40	49
Bottles	24	240	120	96	216	960	1,176

When he finishes, he looks unsure and asks, "Did I do it right?"

2. Review Harvey's ratio table solution and explain each entry.

The next time you see Harvey for tutoring, he pulls some notes from his backpack and says, "Remember that problem about the bottles of lemonade that we did last time? Well, some of my friends did it in different ways. They tried to explain what they did, but I got confused. I know that they got the same answer I did, but I think they did the problem wrong."

Harvey shows you Sean's solution using a ratio table and says, "Sean used a ratio table like I did, but this is what he put down. Is Sean right?"

Crates	1	50	49
Bottles	24	1,200	1,176

3. How would you explain Sean's reasoning to Harvey?

Harvey shows you Sandra's and Hattie's solutions for the lemonade problem, 24 × 49.

Sandra worked the problem like this:

Crates	1	9	40	49
Bottles	24	216	960	1,176

Hattie worked the problem like this:

$$
\begin{array}{r}
24 \\
\times\ 49 \\
\hline
216 \\
960 \\
\hline
1,176
\end{array}
$$

Harvey says, "Sandra and Hattie say that they did the same thing. But Sandra used a ratio table, and Hattie used something that looked totally different. How can these two things be the same?"

4. How are Sandra's and Hattie's ways of multiplying 24 × 49 the same? How are they different?

Hattie used a standard **algorithm** to calculate 24 × 49. An algorithm is a predetermined set of rules used to perform computations. The word comes from the name of an Arabic scientist, al-Khwarizmi, who lived in the ninth century.

Harvey also shows you Clarence's solution. Clarence lists four different multiplication problems. Harvey seems really confused and says, "Look at what Clarence did! I know this can't be right!"

5. How would you explain to Harvey that Clarence's method is a legitimate way to multiply 24 × 49?

Area model

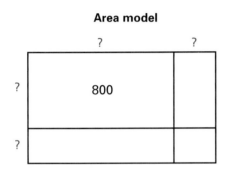

6. If you haven't used it in your answer to problem 5, show how to use the area model to multiply 24 × 49.

7. a. Which of the multiplication methods presented on pages 164 and 165 do you prefer? Explain.

b. Show how to find the product of 28 × 36 using two different methods. You can use any two you prefer.

Division

Sometime in early March, Harvey comes to the tutoring session very upset. He says, "Just when I figured out multiplication, they change the problems. Now they are making us do division!"

You assure him that he will be able to do division problems as easily as he can now do multiplication problems. You suggest that since he likes to use ratio tables to multiply, he may be able to use them to divide. Harvey decides to try it. He reads this problem from his book.

A stapler factory can pack 32 staplers in a standard box. A large company orders 2,000 staplers. How many boxes do you need to fill the order?

Harvey makes this ratio table.

Boxes	1	2	20	60	62
Staplers	32	64	640	1,920	1,984

Harvey finishes his work and says, "The factory has to pack and ship 62 boxes and then figure out how to send 16 more staplers. Or they could just call the people at the company and ask them whether they want 62 or 63 boxes."

Study Harvey's ratio table.

8. How did Harvey find that 60 boxes would hold 1,920 staplers?

Harvey asks you how you would do the problem. You tell him that you would do it mentally. Suppose you shared this mental strategy with Harvey.

One box holds 32 staplers.
One hundred boxes hold 3,200 staplers.

Fifty boxes   hold   1,600 staplers.
Ten boxes   hold   320 staplers.
So **sixty boxes** hold   1,920 staplers.

I still need to pack 80 staplers.
Two more boxes will hold 64 staplers, but there will still be 16 of the 2,000 staplers left to pack.

Just then, Harvey's father comes to take Harvey home. Harvey is so excited about being able to do division problems that he gives his dad the stapler factory problem to see how his father would do it. His father picks up a pencil and writes out the following.

$$
\begin{array}{r}
62 \\
32\overline{)2000} \\
-192 \\
\hline
80 \\
-64 \\
\hline
16
\end{array}
$$

9. a. Compare the mental strategy with Harvey's ratio table strategy and his Dad's strategy. Describe any similarities and differences among these strategies.

   b. Which method do you usually use to solve this kind of problem?

Multiplication and division are very closely related. In fact, for every multiplication problem, there are at least two related division problems. You will explore this relationship using the multiplication problem Harvey read from his book.

> A crate of Lemon Drop lemonade contains 24 bottles. If a supermarket manager bought 49 full crates, how many bottles did she buy?

The number sentence that matches this situation is $24 \times 49 = 1{,}176$.

10. Can the number sentence also be $49 \times 24 = 1{,}176$? Why or why not?

You can also think about the crates and the bottles like this:

> "There are 1,176 bottles of lemonade in crates.
> 24 bottles fill up each crate."

That means that there are 49 crates filled up.

The number sentence that matches this situation is $1{,}176 \div 24 = 49$.

11. Another related number sentence is $1{,}176 \div 49 = 24$. Write a story about the crates and bottles to match this number sentence.

Fraction Operations

In the town where Harvey lives, each city block is about $\frac{1}{8}$ of a mile long. Here is a double number line showing the relationship between city blocks and miles.

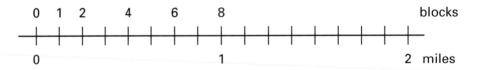

12. a. Harvey lives forty blocks from the mall. How many miles is Harvey's home from the mall? How did you figure this out?

b. Explain how $40 \times \frac{1}{8}$ is related to the home-to-mall situation.

c. Show how to use the ratio table to calculate $40 \times \frac{1}{8}$.

Blocks	1			
Miles	$\frac{1}{8}$			

13. **a.** Harvey lives $3\frac{1}{2}$ miles from school. How many blocks does Harvey live from school? How did you figure this out?

    b. Explain how $3\frac{1}{2} \div \frac{1}{8}$ is related to the school-to-home situation.

To calculate $3\frac{1}{4} \div \frac{1}{8}$, you can make up a context problem like the following.

How many city blocks of $\frac{1}{8}$ mile are there in $3\frac{1}{4}$ miles? Or

how many times does $\frac{1}{8}$ mile fit into $3\frac{1}{4}$ miles?

14. **a.** Calculate $3\frac{1}{4} \div \frac{1}{8}$ using this ratio table.

Blocks	1			
Miles	$\frac{1}{8}$			

    b. Calculate $2\frac{1}{2} \div \frac{1}{8}$.

    c. How would you calculate $2\frac{1}{2} \div \frac{1}{6}$?

15. **a.** Harvey's mother made 6 liters of lemonade, and she wants to store it in $\frac{3}{4}$ liter bottles. How many bottles can she fill with lemonade? Show your work.

    b. Make up a context problem that fits with $6 \div \frac{2}{3}$ and find the answer.

To calculate $6 \div \frac{2}{3}$, you can use a ratio table, but Chi likes to use a different strategy.

"$6 \div \frac{2}{3}$ means that I have to figure out how many times $\frac{2}{3}$ fits into 6. So I will rewrite 6 into thirds."

$$6 \div \frac{2}{3} = \frac{18}{3} \div \frac{2}{3}$$
$$= 18 \div 2$$
$$= 9$$

Chi

16. **a.** Explain why $6 = \frac{18}{3}$.

    b. Why can you find the answer of $\frac{18}{3} \div \frac{2}{3}$ by calculating $18 \div 2$?

17. Use Chi's algorithm to calculate:

    a. $6 \div \frac{3}{7} =$

    b. $5 \div \frac{2}{3} =$

    c. $2 \div \frac{4}{5} =$

1. Marge drove 65 miles from Springfield to Boville. She left Springfield at 2:00 P.M. and arrived in Boville at 3:15 P.M. She uses this ratio table to find the average speed for her trip. Explain Marge's method.

Distance (in mi)	65	260	52	
Time (in hours)	$1\frac{1}{4}$	5	1	

2. Instead of writing $1\frac{1}{4}$ hours for the travel time, you can use quarters of an hour or minutes. Find the average speed for Marge's trip using the following ratio tables.

Distance (in mi)	65				
Time (in quarter hours)	5				

Distance (in mi)	65				
Time (in minutes)	75				

BOVILLE   65
MONTELLO   80
ST. CLARE   115

How Fast? (page 2)

3. Use a ratio table to calculate the average speed for each of the following trips.

   a. Departure Time: 8:00 A.M. Arrival Time: 9:30 A.M.
   Distance Traveled: 81 miles

Distance (in mi)					
Time (in)					

   b. Departure Time: 2:00 P.M. Arrival Time: 5:30 P.M.
   Distance Traveled: 140 miles

Distance (in mi)					
Time (in)					

   c. Departure Time: 8:15 A.M. Arrival Time: 10:00 A.M.
   Distance Traveled: 84 miles

Distance (in mi)					
Time (in)					

   d. Departure Time: 9:05 A.M. Arrival Time: 9:55 A.M.
   Distance Traveled: 30 miles

Distance (in mi)					
Time (in)					

   e. Departure Time: 7:30 A.M. Arrival Time: 4:00 P.M.
   Distance Traveled: 170 miles

Distance (in mi)					
Time (in)					

4. The average speed for the trip in part **e** above is very slow. Provide a possible explanation for the slow average speed.

Key to Success

BRITANNICA
Mathematics
in
Context

Level 3

Lesson
Seventeen
Activities

Operations

Funny Zero

In the Lesson 16 Activities, you worked with Harvey on multiplication and division problems. Now you will work with him on the relationship between these operations.

You say to Harvey, "For every multiplication problem, there are two related division problems. For example, you can take $3 \times 7 = 21$ and write $21 \div 3 = 7$."

  1. a. Write the other division statement for $3 \times 7 = 21$.

      b. Write the two division statements for $8 \times 7 = 56$.

      c. Write the two division statements for $1 \times 6 = 6$

      d. What multiplication statements fit $18 \div 6 = 3$?

Next, you ask Harvey to write a division statement for the following situation:

You have six stickers, and you share them with no one. Harvey smiles and says, "I know that! I have six stickers and share them with nobody.

The division statement is $6 \div 0 = 6$. I am sharing them with nobody, so I have all six stickers."

  2. a. What do you think of Harvey's division statement?

      b. Write a multiplication statement related to Harvey's division statement. What is unusual?

After thinking about it, you realize that Harvey's answer cannot be right. To help Harvey see that something is wrong with his answer, you ask him to divide 6 by 0 with his calculator.

  3. Divide 6 by 0 on your calculator. What do you get?

Harvey is surprised and asks you, "Why didn't the calculator like my problem?"

You answer, "Good question. Why don't we check it out?"

You now ask Harvey to write division statements for $7 \times 0 = 0$ and $8 \times 0 = 0$. He writes, $0 \div 0 = 7$ and $0 \div 0 = 8$.

4. What is odd about Harvey's division statements?

Harvey smiles and says, "Now I know why my calculator got all confused when I put in $6 \div 0$. But what about my sticker problem? What if I have six stickers, and I share them with nobody?" You tell Harvey he wrote the wrong statement.

5. What division statement should Harvey have written for his sticker problem?

6. Make up a context problem to illustrate why $0 \div 8 = 0$.

Negative Numbers

An airplane is leaving from Amsterdam on a transatlantic flight to Philadelphia.

During the flight, TV screens show the flight path along with data about the altitude of the plane and the temperature outside the plane.

Bethany is interested in the temperatures and makes these notes:

Altitude (in ft)	Outside Air Temperature (in °C)
Amsterdam, 0	16
1,000	14
5,000	6

7. a. At what altitude will the temperature drop below zero?

   b. Write a rule describing what happens to the temperature as you go up.

   c. Use your rule to predict the temperature at an altitude of 30,000 feet.

Bethany wrote down 16 + 30 × –2.

8. Explain how this calculation fits problem 7c.

Bethany's calculation uses the multiplication 30 × –2.

9. a. Find the product of 30 × –2.

   b. Thinking of the tutoring session in problem 1, write two division statements related to this multiplication statement.

The airplane changed altitude, and the temperature dropped by 10 degrees. Bethany wants to figure out how the altitude of the airplane changed.

10. a. How would you explain to Bethany that she can find the change in altitude by calculating (10 ÷ 2) × 1,000 feet?

   b. Explain that she can also find the change in altitude by calculating (–10 ÷ –2) × 1,000 feet.

11. Copy and complete the following calculations.

   a.
   ```
   10 ÷ 2 =
    5 ÷ 2 =
    0 ÷ 2 =
   –5 ÷ 2 =
   –10 ÷ 2 =
   ```

   b.
   ```
   –10 ÷ –2 =
    –5 ÷ –2 =
     0 ÷ –2 =
     5 ÷ –2 =
    10 ÷ –2 =
   ```

You may remember the four rules for multiplication of positive and negative numbers. Two of the rules are:

positive × positive = positive

positive × negative = negative

12. What are the other two rules for multiplication?

13. Copy and complete this tree.

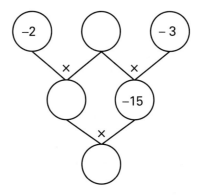

There are also four rules for division. One rule is:

positive ÷ positive = positive

14. What are the other three rules for division? Illustrate each rule with an example.

15. Copy this tree. Perform the division operations from left to right.

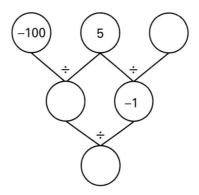

16. Refer to the trees in problems 13 and 15. Why do you have to work from left to right in the tree in problem 15, and why is that not necessary in the tree in problem 13?

Number Properties

If you finish a job in five hours, you will get three dollars per hour. If you finish a job in three hours, you will get five dollars per hour.

17. What do you think of this offer?

In a context problem, 5 × 3 can mean something different from 3 × 5, but the product is the same.

The statement 3 × 5 = 5 × 3 illustrates the **commutative property of multiplication**.

18. For which operations is the commutative property not valid? Justify your conclusions.

Dirk works at a restaurant on weekends. He earns $4\frac{1}{2}$ dollars per hour. This weekend on Saturday, he worked 5 hours, and on Sunday, he worked 3 hours.

19. a. How much money did he earn on Saturday? How much on Sunday?

   b. How much did Dirk earn on both days combined?

   To answer 19b, Dirk wrote:

   $5 \times 4\frac{1}{2} + 3 \times 4\frac{1}{2} = 8 \times 4\frac{1}{2}$.

   c. Explain each number in this equality, and see if $8 \times 4\frac{1}{2}$ matches your answer for 19 b.

Dirk decided to add 5 and 3 first and then multiply the result by $4\frac{1}{2}$, instead of multiplying $5 \times 4\frac{1}{2}$ and $3 \times 4\frac{1}{2}$ first, and then add the results.

Dirk's strategy illustrates the **distributive property of multiplication (over addition)**.

Many people use the distributive property without realizing they are using it.

◆

Which Costs Less?

1. Soft Tunes and Audio Auction feature the same items but offer different discounts. Without using your calculator, circle which store has the lower sale price for each item featured. Be prepared to justify your selection.

Item	Regular Price	Soft Tunes Discount	Audio Auction Discount
CD Player	$360	25%	$70 off
Portable Stereo/ CD Player	$270	$33\frac{1}{3}\%$	$100 off
Speakers	$548	20%	$100 off
Stereo Cabinet	$598	15%	$100 off

2. Describe two ways to find 20% of $450.

3. Calculate each of the following.

a. 20% of $125

b. 25% of $844

c. $33\frac{1}{3}\%$ of $180

d. 10% of $976

e. 15% of $620

f. 25% of $320

g. 10% of $529

h. $66\frac{2}{3}\%$ of $690

i. $33\frac{1}{3}\%$ of $219

◆ **Name** _____ **Date** _____ **Class** _____

On the Number Line

For each number line, find the number indicated by the arrow. For each number line, the marks are the same distance apart.

1.

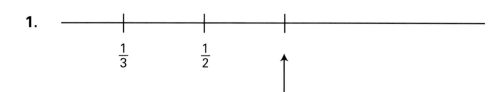

_____

2.

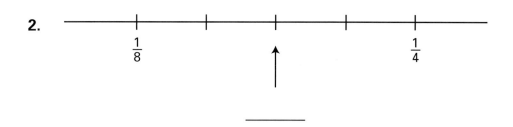

_____

3.

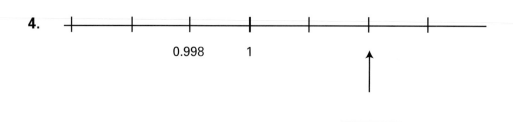

_____

4.

_____

Key to Success

BRITANNICA
Mathematics
in
Context

Level 3

Lesson
Eighteen
Activities

Tessellations

Triangles Forming Triangles

Activity

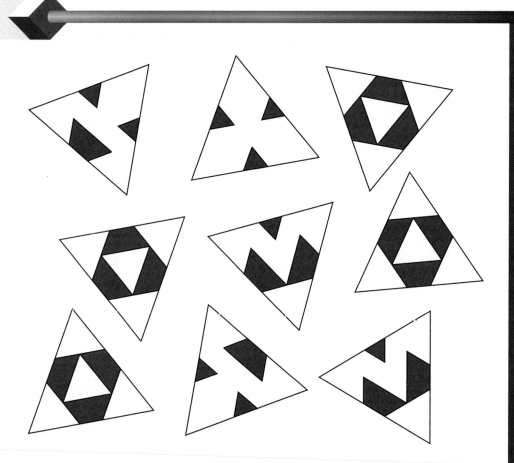

Cut out the nine triangles on **Student Activity Sheet 1**.

- Use all nine triangles to form one large triangle.

- Rearrange the nine triangles to form one large triangle so you form a black triangle whenever two triangles meet.

- Rearrange the nine triangles to form a symmetric pattern. How can you tell your arrangement is symmetric?

A **tessellation** is a repeating pattern that completely covers a larger figure using smaller shapes. Here are two tessellations covering a triangle and a **rhombus**.

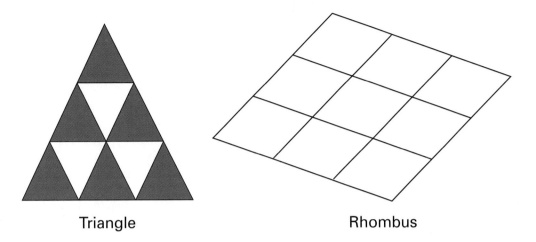

Triangle   Rhombus

1. **a.** How does the area of the large triangle compare to the area of the rhombus?

   b. The triangle consists of nine **congruent** triangles. What does the word *congruent* mean?

   c. The rhombus consists of a number of congruent rhombuses. How many?

   d. You can use the blue and white triangles to cover or tessellate the rhombus. How many of these triangles do you need to tessellate the large rhombus?

   e. Can you tessellate a triangle with 16 congruent triangles? If so, make a sketch. If not, explain why not.

Here is a large triangle tessellation.

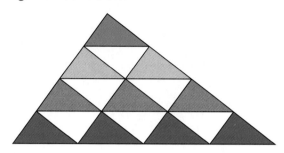

You can break it down by cutting rows along **parallel lines**.

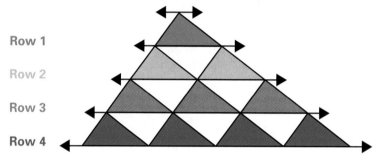

Row 1

Row 2

Row 3

Row 4

These lines form one **family of parallel lines**. There are other families of parallel lines.

2. How many different families of parallel lines are in this large triangle?

Here is the triangle cut along a different family of parallel lines.

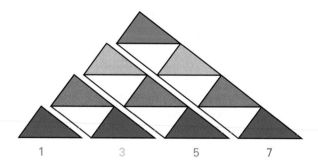

1   3   5   7

3. a. Explain the numbers below each row.

b. Explain what the sequence of numbers 1, 4, 9, 16 has to do with the numbers below each row.

c. Lily copied this tessellation but decided to add more rows. She used 49 small triangles. How many triangles are in Lily's last row?

It's All in the Family

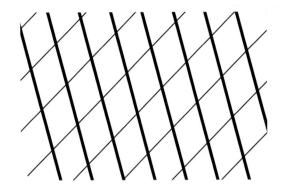

Here is a drawing, made with two families of parallel lines. It is the beginning of a tessellation of parallelograms.

4. a. On **Student Activity Sheet 2**, draw in a third family of parallel lines to form a triangle tessellation.

   b. Are the resulting triangles congruent? Why or why not?

   c. Did everyone in your class draw the same family of parallel lines?

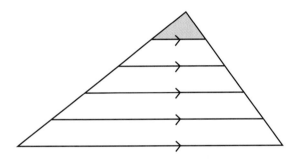

You can use one small triangle to make a triangle tessellation. All you need to do is draw the three families of parallel lines that match the direction of each side of the triangle.

This large triangle shows one family of parallel lines.

5. a. Here's how to finish this triangle tessellation. On **Student Activity Sheet 2**, use a straightedge to draw the other two families of parallel lines.

   b. How many small triangles are along each edge?

   c. How many small triangles tessellate the large triangle?

6. a. If the triangle in problem 5 had ten rows, how many triangles would be along each edge?

   b. How many small triangles would tessellate a triangle with ten rows?

7. a. Think about a large triangle that has *n* rows in each direction. How many small triangles would be along each edge of the large triangle?

   b. Write a formula for the total number of triangles to tessellate a triangle with *n* rows.

Laura used one triangle to make rows of congruent triangles.

 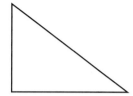  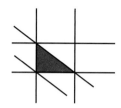

She noticed very interesting things happen.

- Rows form parallel lines in three different directions.

- There is the same number of small triangles along each edge.

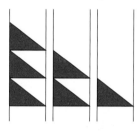 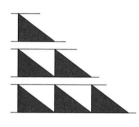 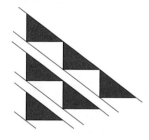

8. a. Make up your own large triangle tessellation using one small triangle.

   b. Verify that the formula you found in problem 7b works for this tessellation.

Tessellations can make beautiful designs. Here is a tessellation design based on squares. This tessellation consists of eight pieces using only two different shapes.

9. a. How many total pieces do you need to make each of these tessellation designs? How many different shapes do you need?

i.  **ii.** 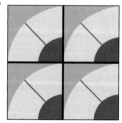 **iii.**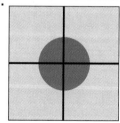

   b. Design your own tessellation, based on squares, which consists of 16 pieces using exactly four different shapes.

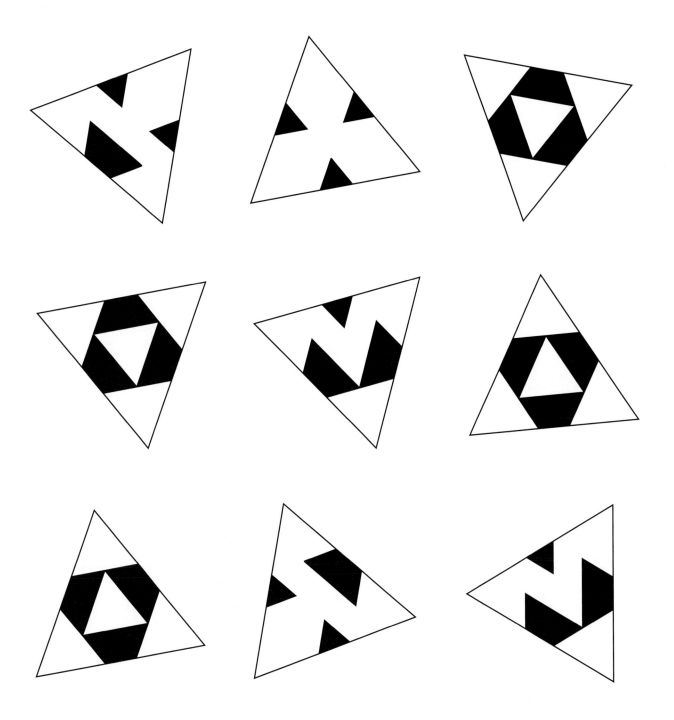

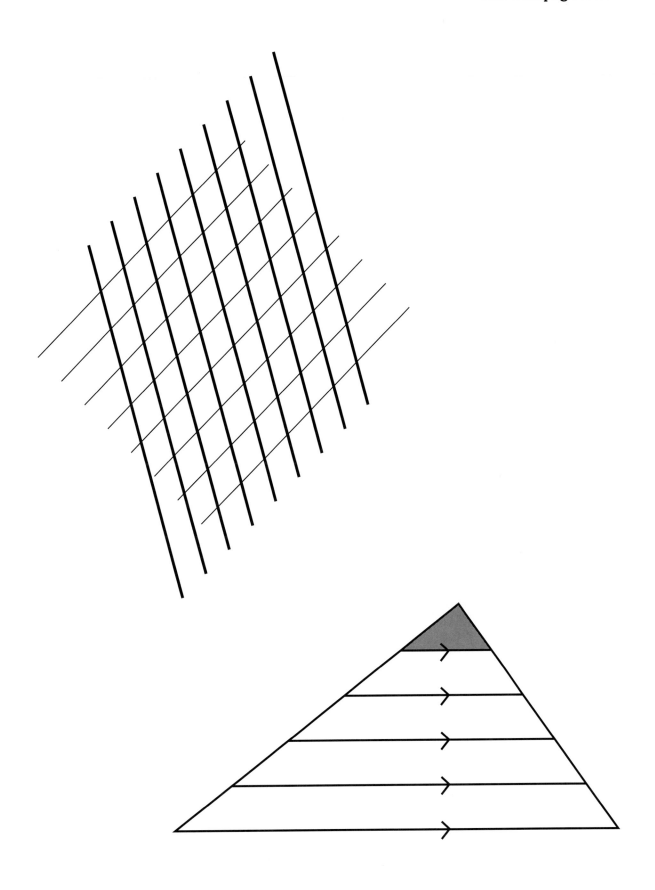

Here is a scaled drawing of a beautiful square terrace. Each tile is imported from Italy and measures 1 m by 1 m.

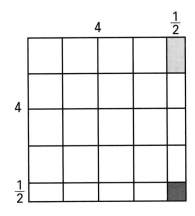

1. **a.** A small part of a tile is colored light gray. What fractional part of a tile is this piece?

   b. And the part in the bottom right corner?

   c. Use this drawing to calculate the area of the whole terrace.

2. A smaller square terrace has side lengths of $3\frac{1}{2}$ m. Calculate the area of this terrace. Show your work.

3. **a.** On the drawing, label the area of each of the parts.

   b. What is $(7\frac{1}{2})^2 = ?$

4. **a.** On the drawing, label the area of each of the parts.

   b. What is $(6\frac{1}{3})^2 = ?$

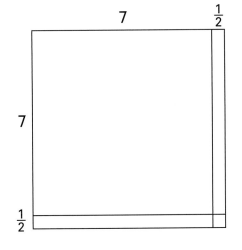

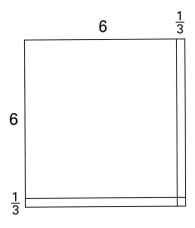

Area Model (page 2)

5. Write the multiplication problem represented by this rectangle.

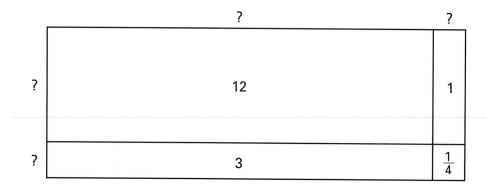

6. Write the problem represented by this square.

?	0.75
0.75	0.25

7. Make up your own area model problem. Ask a classmate to solve your problem.

Key to Success

Level 3

Lesson
Nineteen
Activities

Angles and Triangles

Parallel Lines and Angles

A family of parallel lines is a set of lines that are parallel to one another.

1. **a.** On **Student Activity Sheet 1**, use the symbols ● and ○ and **X** to mark all angles that have the same measure.

   b. Use your drawing to explain why ● + ○ + **X** = 180°.

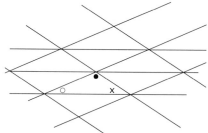

Activity

Starting with a Semicircle

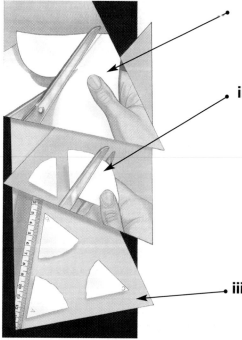

i. Cut a semicircle from a piece of paper. You don't have to be very precise, but it helps to use the edge of the paper for the straight side of the semicircle.

ii. Select a point along the straight side of the semicircle. Draw two lines through this point. Before cutting, label each section near the point using the letters *A*, *B*, and *C*. Cut the semicircle into three pieces.

iii. Create triangle *ABC* by rearranging the three pieces. It helps to have the rounded edges inward. Sketch the triangle.

iv. Now move the pieces a little farther apart and closer together to make larger and smaller triangles. Sketch each of these triangles.

v. Repeat the steps using a different semicircle. Describe your results. Keep these pieces handy for future work.

2. Can you cut a semicircle into three pieces that will not form a triangle? Explain. Assume that the pieces were cut using the directions from this activity.

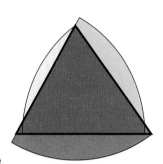

3. From the activity, you might have discovered some geometric properties about angles and triangles. Summarize your discoveries in your notebook.

This drawing represents a geometric property about three angles cut from a semicircle. The sum of the three angles is 180°.

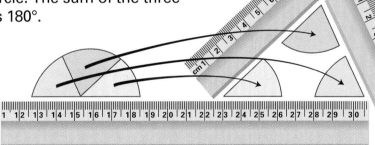

4. Use this information to rewrite the geometric property you described in problem 3.

Find the semicircle pieces from the previous activity.

5. Select three angle pieces whose measures total more than 180°. Try to make a triangle with them. Is this possible? How can you be sure?

6. Select three angles whose measures total less than 180°. Try to make a triangle with them. Is this possible? How can you be sure?

Here is a drawing much like the previous drawing.

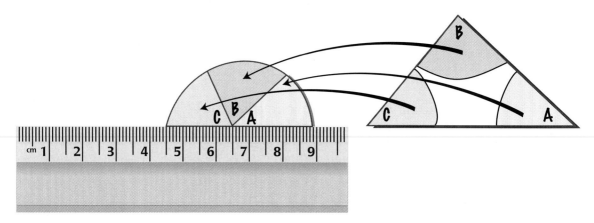

7. a. What geometric property of triangles is pictured?

 b. Reflect Describe how these two properties and the two pictures are related.

Here is triangle *PQR*.

P, *Q*, and *R* are the names of the vertices of the triangle.

∠*P* is a shorter notation for the angle at **vertex** *P*.

You can replace the word *triangle* with a △ symbol. Instead of writing *triangle PQR*, you can write △ *PQR*.

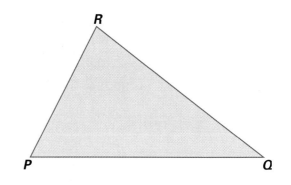

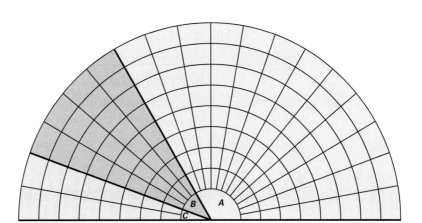

Here are three angles: ∠A, ∠B, and ∠C.

They are drawn in a semicircle that has been subdivided into equal parts. They can be cut apart and put together to form △ABC.

8. a. What are the measures of ∠A, ∠B, and ∠C?

b. Start with a line segment that is 10 cm long and label its ends A and C.

c. ∠A occurs at point A. Draw ∠A on your piece of paper.

d. Finish drawing △ABC.

e. Is it necessary to use the measures of all three angles to complete your triangle? Explain why or why not.

f. There are many different triangles with the same three angle measures you drew in part **d**. Draw another △ABC, this time with a different length for side AC. Compare your triangle to a classmate's drawing. Describe any similarities and differences among the three triangles.

Triangles and Angles

Here is an **isosceles triangle**. The slashes on the sides show which two sides are of equal length.

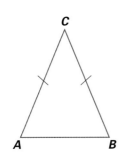

9. a. In △ABC, name the shortest side. Name the angle opposite this shortest side.

b. Name the angles opposite sides AC and BC.

c. Describe any relationship between the two angles.

d. Which angle is smaller: ∠A or ∠C? How can you be sure without measuring it directly?

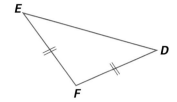

10. **a.** In △*DEF*, name the longest side and name the angle opposite the longest side.

    b. What do you know about the sides that are opposite the other two angles? Describe any relationship between the angles.

Activity

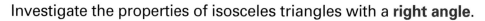

Investigate the properties of isosceles triangles with a **right angle**.

11. **a.** Fold the isosceles triangle in half. What geometric property about isosceles triangles did you illustrate?

    b. Investigate the properties of an isosceles triangle with a right angle. How is this isosceles triangle different from any isosceles triangle? How is it the same?

12. What can you conclude about the angles of an **equilateral triangle**? Be prepared to use your equilateral triangle to demonstrate your conclusions.

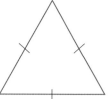

13. Copy and complete the sentences describing the angles of isosceles and equilateral triangles.

    In an isosceles triangle,…

    In an equilateral triangle,…

1. a. Use the symbols ● and ○ and **x** to mark all angles that have the same measure.

　　b. Use your drawing to explain why the sum of the degrees of ● and ○ and **x** = 180°.

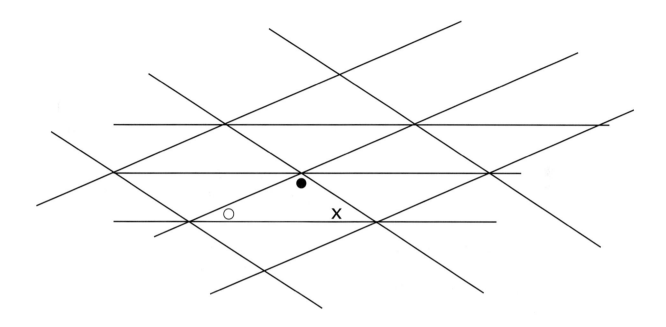

Name _____ Date _____ Class _____

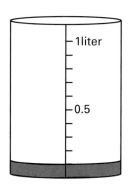

A Little about Liters

Here is a graduated cylinder. You can measure the volume of a liquid by reading the water level. The markings on the cylinder indicate that you can measure up to one liter of liquid.

1. What is the water level of this cylinder? What is the volume of the liquid?

2. What interval markings would you want on the cylinder if you had to measure 0.07 liter of liquid?

Milliliters (ml), centiliters (cl), deciliters (dl), and **liters(l)** are metric units used to measure liquid volume.

milli means one-thousandth one milliliter = $\frac{1}{1000}$ liter

centi means one-hundredth one centiliter = $\frac{1}{100}$ liter

deci means one-tenth one deciliter = $\frac{1}{10}$ liter

---

3. A tin can holds 0.33 liter of lemonade. Mark the level on this graduated cylinder to show 0.33 liter of lemonade.

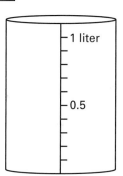

4. a. How much is 0.33 liter in deciliters?

0.33 liter = ____ deciliters

b. How much is 0.33 liter in centiliters?

0.33 liter = ____ centiliters

c. How much is 0.33 liter in milliliters?

0.33 liter = ____ milliliters

5. a. Draw the level of the liquid in each cylinder to show the given amount.

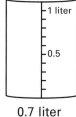   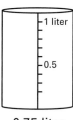

0.7 liter   0.07 liter   0.05 liter   0.75 liter

b. Order the amounts of liquid shown in part **a** from smallest to largest.

Name _____ Date _____ Class_____

The Meter

Around 1800, the meter was designed to be one ten-millionth of the distance between the Equator and the North Pole.

1. According to this design, how far is the North Pole from the Equator in meters? And in kilometers?

Several signs in Wisconsin and upper Michigan mark the halfway point between the Equator and the North Pole. There are two different ways to define halfway between the Equator and the North Pole. Here you see an example of each.

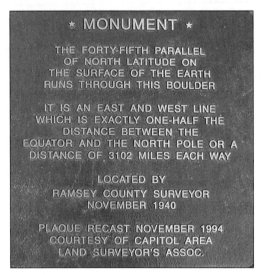
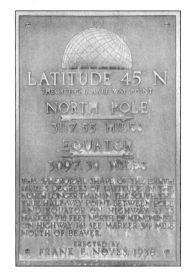

2. **a.** What are the two different ways to define halfway between the Equator and the North Pole?

   b. Use the information on each sign to calculate the distance, in miles, from the North Pole to the Equator.

You have the distance between the Equator and the North Pole measured with two different units, a meter and a mile.

3. Use your answers to problems 1 and 2 to find two relationships between a meter and a mile.

Today, the meter is defined precisely; one mile is about 1609.344 meters.

4. Today, what is the precise distance from the equator to the North Pole? Calculate the distance in meters and in kilometers.

Key to Success

BRITANNICA
Mathematics
in
Context

Level 3

Lesson
Twenty
Activities

Sides and Angles

Squares and Triangles

In this section, you will use squares to create triangles.

This figure illustrates how three squares form a triangle.

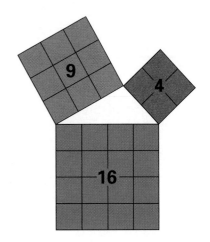

1. a. How long is each side of this triangle? How do you know?

  b. Find the largest angle of this triangle.

Triangles can be classified like this: If the largest angle of a triangle is acute, the triangle is called an **acute triangle**.

  c. Define **right triangle** and **obtuse triangle**.

Sylvia notices a geometric property: You can find the largest angle of a triangle opposite the longest side.

  d. Does this property apply to the triangle in the picture above?

2. a. Draw a scalene right triangle. Using the same color, show the triangle's largest angle and longest side. Does Sylvia's property apply to this triangle?

  b. Using a different color, show the triangle's smallest angle and shortest side.

  c. **Reflect** Describe another geometric property related to the right triangle. Write about the geometric properties of an isosceles right triangle.

3. a. Draw an acute triangle and investigate whether Sylvia's property also applies to this triangle.

  b. Does the geometric property apply to the acute triangle? Describe where you would find the smallest angle of the triangle.

Making Triangles from Squares

For this activity, you need:

- two copies each of **Student Activity Sheet 1** and **Student Activity Sheet 2**;

- scissors; and

- paper.

- Use two copies of **Student Activity Sheet 1** to cut out a sequence of ten white squares representing the first ten perfect square numbers. On each square, write the number of tiles used to make each square. Do the same using two copies of **Student Activity Sheet 2**.

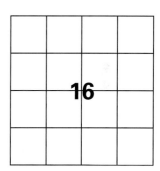

- For this activity, you will use one white square and two gray squares to form different triangles. The white square will always form the longest side of the triangle. The two gray squares will always form the shorter sides of the triangle.

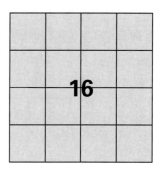

- Select one white square and two gray squares that can be arranged to make a triangle. Note that each gray square has to be smaller than the white square. Record your results in a table like this. Problem 1 is recorded.

Total Number of Gray Tiles	Total Number of White Tiles	Classification of the Triangle According to Its Largest Angle
4 + 9 = 13	16	obtuse

- Repeat this process for at least five more triangles. Make sure to represent all types of triangles: acute, obtuse, and right.

4. a. Compare your results of the activity to a classmate's results. Describe any patterns in your results.

   b. Describe any special relationship between the white and gray tiles of a right triangle.

Select two gray squares—one with 25 tiles and one with 64 tiles.

5. a. Find the size of a white square that is needed to create an acute triangle.

   b. Find the size of a white square that is needed to create an obtuse triangle.

The Pythagorean Theorem

> If a triangle has a right angle, then the square on the longest side has the same area as the other two combined.

About 2,500 years ago in Greece, there lived a famous mathematician, scientist, and philosopher named Pythagoras.

Pythagoras described a way of constructing right angles and the relationship among the areas of the three squares. This relationship is described by the **Pythagorean theorem**.

This figure shows a right triangle and three squares.

6. Find the area of the white square. Show your work.

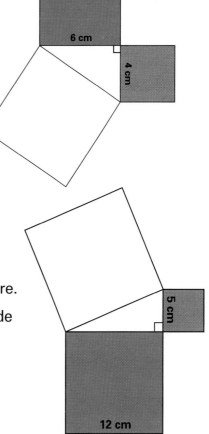

6 cm

4 cm

7. **a.** Find the area of the largest square.

   b. Find the length of the longest side of the triangle.

5 cm

12 cm

You can find the length of the sides of a square by "unsquaring" the area; for example:

The length of the sides of this square is the **square root** *of 5*.

The square root of 5 is written √5.

You can use a calculator to estimate the length for the square root of 5.

√5 ≈ 2.24

Therefore, each side of the square is about 2.24 cm.

8. a. Look back at the white square in problem 6. Use the square root notation to show the length of the side of the square.

   b. Use your calculator to approximate the length of the sides of the white square. Round your answer to one decimal place.

This figure shows a right triangle with short sides of 3 cm and 5 cm. There are many ways to find the length of side *AB*.

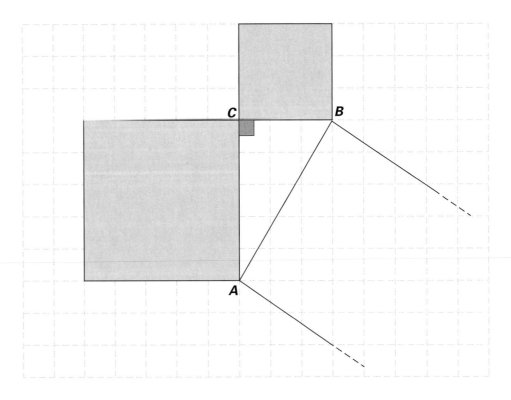

Here is one way to find the length of side *AB*.

area of the square on side *AC* = ...

area of the square on side *BC* = ...

+
_____

....

area of the square on side *AB* = ...

so *AB* = ...

9. Find the length of side *AB*. Round your answer to the nearest tenth.

Here are two right triangles.

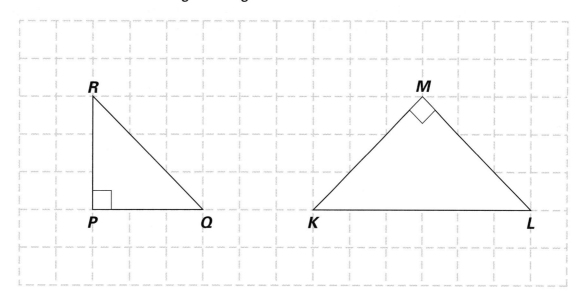

10. **a.** Find the side lengths of △*PQR*. Show your work.

b. Find the side lengths of △*KLM*. Show your work.

Key to Success